REVISE EDEXCEL GCSE
History
Specification B Schools History Project
REVISION WORKBOOK
Support

Authors: Nigel Bushnell and Cathy Warren

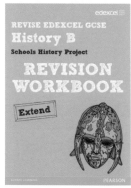

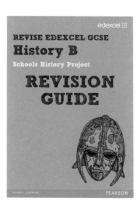

THE REVISE EDEXCEL SERIES
Available in print or online

Online editions for all titles in the Revise Edexcel series are available Autumn 2012.

Presented on our ActiveLearn platform, you can view the full book and customise it by adding notes, comments and weblinks.

Print editions

History B Support Revision Workbook	9781446905104
History B Extend Revision Workbook	9781446905074
History B Revision Guide	9781446905142

Online editions

History B Support Revision Workbook	9781446904985
History B Extend Revision Workbook	9781446905159
History B Revision Guide	9781446905166

Print and online editions are also available for History Specification A Support and Extend Workbooks and Revision Guide.

This Revision Workbook is designed to complement your classroom and home learning, and to help you prepare for the exam. It does not include all the content and skills needed for the complete course. It is designed to work in combination with Edexcel's main GCSE History 2009/2012 Series.

To find out more visit:
www.pearsonschools.co.uk/edexcelgcsehistoryrevision

LWAYS LEARNING

PEARSON

Published by Pearson Education Limited, Edinburgh Gate, Harlow, Essex, CM20 2JE.

www.pearsonschoolsandfecolleges.co.uk

Text © Pearson Education Limited 2012
Designed and typeset by Juice Creative Limited, Hertfordshire and Jerry Udall
Cover illustration by Miriam Sturdee

The rights of Nigel Bushnell and Cathy Warren to be identified as authors of this work have been asserted
by them in accordance with the Copyright, Designs and Patents Act 1988.

First published 2012

16 15 14 13 12
10 9 8 7 6 5 4 3 2 1

British Library Cataloguing in Publication Data
A catalogue record for this book is available from the British Library

ISBN 978 1 446 90510 4

Printed in Malaysia (CTP-VP)

Acknowledgements
Picture Credits
The publisher would like to thank the following for their kind permission to reproduce their photographs:

akg-images Ltd: Coll. F. Kunst & Geschichte 11; **British Library Images Online**: 7; **Corbis**: David
Pollack 67, Gideon Mendel 9, Peter Aprahamian 68; **John Bartlett**: 72; **Mary Evans Picture Library**:
Illustrated London News 13, 69

All other images © Pearson Education

Written Sources
We are grateful to the following for permission to reproduce copyright material: Extract on page 71
adapted from `An account of the 1984 Miners' Strike', http:// archiveshub.ac.uk/features/mar04.shtml.
Reproduced by kind permission of The South Wales Coalfield Collection, Swansea University.

Every effort has been made to contact copyright holders of material reproduced in this book. Any
omissions will be rectified in subsequent printings if notice is given to the publishers.

In order to ensure that this resource offers high-quality support for the associated Edexcel qualification,
it has been through a review process by the awarding organisation to confirm that it fully covers the
teaching and learning content of the specification or part of a specification at which it is aimed, and
demonstrates an appropriate balance between the development of subject skills, knowledge and
understanding, in addition to preparation for assessment.

While the publishers have made every attempt to ensure that advice on the qualification and its
assessment is accurate, the official specification and associated assessment guidance materials are the
only authoritative source of information and should always be referred to for definitive guidance.

No material from an endorsed revision workbook will be used verbatim in any assessment set by Edexcel.

Endorsement of a revision workbook does not mean that the revision workbook is required to achieve
this Edexcel qualification, nor does it mean that it is the only suitable material available to support the
qualification, and any resource lists produced by the awarding organisation shall include this and other
appropriate resources.

Contents

BBC - GCSE Bitesize - Schools History Project

Introduction

This workbook has been written to help you practise your exam skills as you prepare for your GCSE History exams for Unit 1, Unit 2 and Unit 3. You'll find practice for each question type, helping you to understand how to improve your answers.

You'll find answers to the activities at the back of the book, so that you can check whether you're on track after you've completed the activities.

Unit 1 Development Study and Unit 2 Depth Study

This workbook covers the following options for Unit 1 and Unit 2:

- 1A Medicine and treatment
- 1B Crime and punishment
- 2B The American West c.1840–c.1895
- 2C Life in Germany c.1919–c.1945

In these two units, the questions follow a similar pattern, testing similar key historical skills. For that reason in this workbook, we look at each historical skill and the Unit 1 and 2 questions that relate to it together. In the exam papers for both units, you will answer five questions.

Question 1	4 marks	Question 3 or Question 4	12 marks
Question 2	9 marks	Question 5(a) and 5(b) or Question 6(a) and 6(b)	(a) 9 marks and (b) 16 marks

In questions 5(b) and 6(b), there are additional marks for spelling, punctuation and grammar.

The examination paper

In both Unit 1 and Unit 2, the questions follow the same pattern.

You must answer question 1, which is always an inference question worth 4 marks.

Question 2 is worth 9 marks and there is always a choice of two options within the question, for example:

> There were two important developments in medical knowledge during the years 1500-1861. Choose ONE of the boxes below and explain why it was important.
>
> Improvements in knowledge of anatomy
>
> Pasteur's germ theory

You then choose EITHER question 3 or question 4. Each of these is worth 12 marks and they always have some stimulus material – a picture, a brief piece of text, or 3 bullet points. This stimulus material is just to help you get started. It reminds you to cover the whole period, look at both sides of the issue, cover more than one factor etc. However, you need to have enough knowledge to make use of this stimulus material, you can't get marks by just re-writing it in your own words. Ideally you will also add some additional points from your own knowledge.

You then choose EITHER question 5 or question 6. Whichever question you choose, you must answer part (a) AND part (b). Part a is worth 9 marks and is usually a straightforward question asking you to describe a situation or identify the key features. Part (b) is the evaluation question which is worth 16 marks.

Question	Marks	Suitable length of answer (exam booklet)	Time
1	4	8–10 lines	5–7 mins
2	9	1–1½ side	10–12 mins
3 or 4	12	1½–2 sides	15–20 mins
5 or 6	Part (a) 9 Part (b) 16	Part (a) 1 side Part (b) 2–2½ sides	Part (a) 10 mins Part (b) 25 mins

Unit 3 Source Enquiry

This workbook covers the following options in Unit 3.

- 3A The transformation of surgery c.1845–c.1918
- 3B Protest, law and order in the twentieth century

You'll find the sources for option 3A on pages 71–72 and the sources for option 3B on pages 73–74. The questions and activities in this workbook will relate to those sources. There are five questions in Unit 3 and you should answer all five. The table below shows which source skill is being tested in each question as well as where you will be marked on your spelling, punctuation and grammar. On pages 68–69, each question type is explained, followed by the sources and the examples and activities for 3A and 3B.

Question 1	6 marks	Inference	Pages 76–81
Question 2	8 marks	Portrayal	Pages 76–81
Question 3	10 marks	Cross-referencing	Pages 82–86
Question 4	10 marks	Evaluation of sources	Pages 87–93
Question 5	16 marks + 3 marks	Reaching a judgement Spelling, punctuation and grammar	Pages 94–100

The examination paper

Unit 3 is slightly different. Each question focuses on a specific skill. You have no choice and you must answer all five questions.

Question	Marks	Suitable length of answer (exam booklet)	Time
1 inference	6	²/₃–1 side	5–7 mins
2 portrayal	8	1 side	10 mins
3 cross-referencing	10	2 sides	15–20 mins
4 evaluation of sources	10	1½ sides	12–15 mins
5 reaching a judgement	16	2–2½ sides	25–30 mins

Inference questions

The first question in both Unit 1 and Unit 2 is an **inference** question. An inference means something that is not actually said or shown in the source but which you can work out from the details of the source.

In other words...

An example of an inference is that if you see someone going into several shops and in each one they ask to see the manager and hand over a letter and their CV, you could **infer** that they are looking for a job.

How do I answer inference questions?

Unit 1 focuses on change and continuity over time. In Unit 1 you will therefore need to make an inference about **change**, based on **two** given sources.

In Unit 2 you will need to make an inference from just **one** given source.

When answering the inference questions in Units 1 and 2, use only the source(s) – you do not need to use any additional own knowledge!

How will I be marked?

The inference questions in both Unit 1 and Unit 2 are worth 4 marks. The mark scheme in both units spreads the marks over two levels:

- Level 1 (1–2 marks): the answer makes an inference but does not show which details of the source(s) have been used to work out the inference OR the answer identifies relevant points from the source(s) but doesn't explain what inference has been made.

- Level 2 (3–4 marks): the answer makes an inference and supports it with details from the source(s).

You need to look at the source(s), then make an inference AND support your inference by using details from the source(s).

If you are studying Medicine in Unit 1, go to page 7. If you are studying Crime, go to page 9.

If you are studying The American West in Unit 2, go to page 11. If you are studying Life in Germany, go to page 13.

Remember

- Make sure you say what you have worked out (inferred) from the source details.

- Explain which details of the source you used to make the inference.

- The question is about the inference. DON'T write a long description of details in the source.

1A Medicine and treatment

Unit 1 focuses on change and continuity over time. Therefore in Unit 1, question 1 always asks you to make inferences about change. For example:

> What can you learn from Sources A and B about changes in nursing in the period between the Middle Ages and the start of the twentieth century? Explain your answer, using these sources. (4 marks)

Source A: An illustration from the Middle Ages, showing a housewife and her maid preparing medicine for the man lying ill in bed.

Source B: From a letter written by William Rathbone to Liverpool nurses in 1901.

> As nurses, you are not inferior servants doing inferior work for inferior wages, but trained and skilled workers carrying out intelligently the treatment prescribed by a doctor.

Activity

1. Read the four comments a–d below. Which of them are valid comments about changes in nursing, based on the two sources above? Circle your choices.

   a. Nurses were better trained as a result of the work of Florence Nightingale.

   b. Nursing used to be done by the women of the family but changed to be done by trained nurses.

   c. Nurses were respected more in the twentieth century than in the Middle Ages.

   d. Women made their own medicines to treat the sick during the Middle Ages but in the twentieth century they had less responsibility because the treatment they gave had been prescribed by a doctor.

Now read the example below that demonstrates how one of the comments has been turned into a Level 2 answer.

Answer A

Nursing used to be done by the woman of the family, at home. This is shown in Source A where the man is in bed and the woman is sitting in front of the fire making her own medicine by following a recipe. By the twentieth century nursing had changed to something that was done by trained nurses. This is shown in B where Rathbone tells nurses they are 'not inferior servants ... but trained and skilled workers'.

2. Look again at the four comments a–d about change and find the other comment that is based on the sources. Write two sentences that clearly identify the change from nursing as it is shown in Source A to nursing in Source B. Support this comment by using a detail from each source.

   ....

   ....

   ....

Read Answer B below and complete the following tasks.

3. Underline in blue the details that come from the sources.

4. Underline in red the comment about change.

5. Use the mark scheme on page 6 to decide how many marks you would give it.

Answer B

In Source A, I can see a woman using a recipe book to prepare medicine for the man who is sick and is lying in bed and her maid is helping her. This shows the way that nursing in the Middle Ages was done by the woman of the family, using her own remedies. Rathbone seems to have a lot of respect for the nurses. This is because Florence Nightingale made a lot of changes to the training of nurses and made it a respectable thing to do. This shows that nursing has changed by 1901 and has become a skilled profession which is respected instead of being part of the normal life of a woman.

I would give this .... marks.

Now read the feedback below.

This answer does make an inference about changes in nursing: that it has gone from being something done within the family to something that needs training. The answer makes some use of the sources to explain this inference, so it is Level 2. However, the link between the details and the inference is not clear so it would receive 3 marks rather than 4. The comment about Florence Nightingale is true but it is not based on the sources and therefore gets no marks. Change is the point of the question, but it is not mentioned until the end of the answer.

6. Using this information, write an improved version of Answer A below by focusing on the **changes in nursing**. Only include detail from the sources if it is being used to support your comment.

....

....

....

....

....

....

....

....

Unit 1 is a Development Study, focusing on change and continuity over time.
Therefore question 1 always asks you to make inferences about change. For example:

What can you learn from Sources A and B about changes in riot control in the period from the eighteenth century to the end of the twentieth century? (4 marks)

Source B: Police in riot gear controlling a demonstration in London in 1999.

Source A: A proclamation by King George III in 1780 saying that the army will be used to deal with riots.

A great number of people have gathered together in a riot. It has become necessary to use military force in order to deal with these disturbances, to protect the lives and properties of individuals, and to restore the peace of the country.

Activity

1. Read the four comments a to d below. Which of them are valid comments about changes in riot control, based on the two sources above? Circle your choices.

   a. Riot control is a lot easier in Source B than it was in Source A.

   b. The army used military force to control riots and were likely to injure or kill people whereas in Source B the police weapons are less likely to kill protesters.

   c. Robert Peel started the Metropolitan Police Force in 1829 and they have specially trained groups to deal with different problems.

   d. Controlling riots and protecting property used to be treated as an emergency and done by the army, but in the twentieth century it was done by the police who were trained to deal with riots as part of their normal duties.

Only two of these comments can be supported from the sources. Read the example below of how one of the comments has been turned into a Level 2 answer.

Answer A

The sources show a change in both the people and the methods used to control riots. Source A shows riot control used to be done by the army who would use military force and therefore were likely to be aggressive and injure or kill the protesters. In the twentieth century Source B shows the police dealing with riots and they had been specially trained and equipped for riot control so that they did not use military force and were less likely to kill or injure protesters.

2. Look again at the four comments a–d about change and find the other comment that is based on the sources. Write two sentences that clearly identify the change and support this comment by using a detail from each source.

....

....

....

....

Read Answer B below, then complete the following tasks.

3. Underline in blue the details that come from the sources.

4. Underline in red the comment about change.

5. Use the mark scheme on page 6 to decide how many marks you would give it.

Answer A

In Source A, I can see that the army was used to deal with riots in the eighteenth century. They were used to protect people and property and to restore order and used military force, which would probably injure or kill people. This shows that riot control in the eighteenth century was treated almost like a war and riots were controlled by violence, with the army acting as an emergency force. By the twentieth century, this has changed because the police dealt with riots and they tried to avoid using violence. When the police were first introduced in the nineteenth century they wore a top hat and their coat was blue to make them look different from the army. In Source B the police have been trained to make a defensive wall to prevent the rioters going any further but they are not attacking them.

I would give this .... marks.

Now read the feedback below.

This answer does make an inference about changes in riot control. There is some use of the sources to explain this inference so it is Level 2. However, the link between the details and the inference is not clear so it would receive 3 marks rather than 4. The comment about the police uniform in the nineteenth century is true but it is not based on the sources and therefore gets no marks. Change is the point of the question, but it is not mentioned until the end of the answer.

6. Using this information, write an improved version of Answer A by focusing on the **changes in riot control** and only including detail from the sources if it is being used to support your comment.

....

....

....

....

....

....

....

....

2B The American West

Unit 2 is a Depth Study which explores a short period of rapid change in history. Here is an example of the type of inference question you will get for Question 1 in Unit 2.

What can you learn from Source A about the Mormon settlement at Salt Lake City, 1895? (4 marks)

Hint

First, remember to look at the caption. This tells you when the photograph was taken. This will help you because you know now that it was taken quite a long time after the Mormons had first arrived at the Great Salt Lake in 1847.

Source A: The Mormon temple in Salt Lake City, 1895.

Activity

1. Read the five inferences a to e below. Which of these are valid inferences that you could make from this particular source? Circle your choices.

   a. Many Mormons used the temple.

   b. It looks like there is a sense of pride in the city because it is well looked after.

   c. The Mormons had escaped religious persecution in the east.

   d. The size of the temple shows that religion was clearly important to the Mormons.

   e. Most of the people living in the city are rich.

2. Now you need to support your inference directly from the source you are using.

   Read the statements below. For each one, tick in the relevant column to show if it:

   A. can be used to support your inference made from this source

   B. is based on own knowledge but not from this source.

	A	B
1. The Mormons had a very skilful leader in Brigham Young.		
2. The temple shows the city was wealthy.		
3. The Mormons had escaped religious persecution in the east.		
4. The Mormon Church shared out land equally among the people.		
5. The Mormons encouraged others to join them by making funds available.		

3. Now write an answer to the question. Remember that the best answers will make a clear inference from this source about the Mormons' success at Salt Lake City AND make a statement to support the inference made which clearly refers to what can be seen in the source about the success of the Mormons at Salt Lake City.

....

....

....

....

....

Read the two answers below.

Answer A

In Source A I can see that the Mormons were successful at Salt Lake City. You can see religion was important because of the size of the temple. Much of this was because of the skills shown by Brigham Young. The Mormons also encouraged many other people with useful skills to join them with the setting up of the Perpetual Emigration Fund. Some people even came from as far away as Europe. Brigham Young's success meant that the US government made him governor for the new state of Utah.

Answer B

The Mormons used a variety of means to ensure that the city at Salt Lake was successful. The city had a large temple in the middle. From the centre of the city land was then shared out to all the people. The city was in the middle of the desert and they could not use water from the Salt Lake. However, the Mormons developed a water system to grow crops and grow trees in the middle of the city.

4. Now give a mark for each student's answer and explain why you have awarded that mark. Remember to use the mark scheme on page 6.

Answer A mark: .... Explanation:	Answer B mark: .... Explanation:

2C Life in Germany

Unit 2 is a Depth Study which explores a short period of rapid change in history.
Here is an example of the type of inference question you will get for question 1 in Unit 2.

> What can you learn from Source A about methods used by the Nazi government to control Germany? (4 marks)

Source A: A photograph of book-burning in central Berlin, May 1933

Hint

First remember to look at the caption. This tells you when and where the photograph was taken. This will help you because you know that it was after Hitler had become Chancellor in January 1933.

Activity

1. Read the five inferences a to e below. Which of these are valid inferences which you could make from this particular source? Circle your choices.

   a. The Nazis were against the Jews and communists.

   b. The Nazis wanted to control what people read.

   c. The Nazis believed in Germany expanding eastwards.

   d. Many Germans were against book-burning.

   e. The Nazis wanted to destroy ideas and beliefs they did not agree with.

2. Now you need to support your inference directly from the source you are using.

   Read the statements below. For each one, tick the relevant column to show if it:

   A. can be used to support your inference made from this source

   B. is based on own knowledge but not from this source.

	A	B
1. Books were burnt as if it were a ceremony with people saluting Hitler.		
2. Books by Jewish authors were publicly burnt.		
3. Books were burnt openly in a city in full view of the public.		
4. Goebbels was Minister of Propaganda and ordered book-burning.		
5. The Nazis also controlled plays, the cinema, radio and newspapers.		

3. Now write a full answer to the question. Remember that the best answers will make a clear inference from this source about methods used by the Nazis to control Germany AND make a statement to support the inference made which clearly refers to what can be seen in the source about Nazi government control.

....

....

....

....

....

Read the two answers below.

Answer A

In Source A I can see that one method used by the Nazis to control Germany was the burning of books which did not agree with the Nazi government's beliefs. These book-burnings were ordered by the Minister for Propaganda and carried out in busy areas in full public view. The burnings were almost like a ceremony or ritual to celebrate the Nazi government and you can see people giving the Nazi salute. This was part of the whole policy of censorship used by the Nazi government, which as well as books also included newspapers, films, plays and music.

Answer B

A method used by the Nazis to control Germany was to control ideas. They did this by using ways to stop ideas which they did not agree with spreading and also by making sure that people only read and heard ideas that the Nazis believed in. One way of doing this was by burning books. People often stood and watched what was going on and some showed their support for Hitler by giving the Nazi salute.

4. Now give a mark for each student's answer and explain why you have awarded that mark. Remember to use the mark scheme on page 6.

Answer A mark: .... Explanation:	Answer B mark: .... Explanation:

Causation questions

How do I answer causation questions?

Causation means looking at the reasons WHY things happen in history – the CAUSES of events and change in history. To answer a causation question you need to EXPLAIN why something happened.

How will I be marked?

In both Unit 1 and Unit 2, any question could ask about causation, except question 1.

- Question 2, question 5(a) and question 6(a) are worth 9 marks.
- Question 3 and question 4 are worth 12 marks.

These causation questions are all marked in the same way, using levels from Level 1 up to Level 3. In a 12-mark question the mark scheme would be as follows:

Level	Marks	Answer
1	1–4	Answer is very general, few details included.
2	5–8	Answer has correct detail but does not show how the details help to answer the specific question.
3	9–12	Answer uses detail to support an explanation.

Make sure you identify each point or reason clearly. It helps if you use words or phrases such as 'because', 'therefore', 'as a result' and 'which meant that'. These all demonstrate that you are explaining the connections between the points you are making.

You could also group different reasons together, for example:

- economic factors (reasons to do with money)
- religious factors (reasons to do with people's beliefs)
- social factors (reasons to do with the way society works and people's attitudes).

We also sometimes identify the role of an individual factor, for example:

- the government (what was organised on a national basis)
- technology (how equipment and machinery affected the situation).

In other words…

If you were asked by your teacher why you were so late for school, you might say:

We had a power cut during the night so I woke up late. And then I couldn't find my phone.

This would be a low Level 2 answer, because it just tells the story of what happened. To improve it, you would need to make it clear that:

- the power cut is the reason why you woke up late – it meant that your alarm clock didn't go off
- you spent so long trying to find your phone that you missed your bus.

1A Medicine and treatment

Unit 1 is a Development Study. Questions on causation in this unit ask why change happened but also why change didn't happen (why there was continuity) or why it took so long for the situation to change. For example:

> Why did it take so long for penicillin to be produced on a large scale? (12 marks)
>
> The following information may help you with your answer:
>
> Alexander Fleming investigated penicillin bacteria in 1928 when it affected a mould he was growing as part of an experiment. He published his findings in an article in 1929.

Activity

1. Read Answer A below. Underline any reasons that you can find in it which explain why it took so long for penicillin to be produced on a large scale. Then check your answer with the mark scheme on page 15.

Answer A

Alexander Fleming discovered penicillin when he came back from holiday and found that a mould he had been growing in a petri dish was being killed off by a new bacteria growing there. He investigated and found that the new bacteria, penicillin, could kill other bacteria. It was an antibiotic which could be used to fight infection. He found that it was killed by stomach acid but he thought it could be used on the skin. However, it was difficult to produce in large quantities so he published his findings in a medical journal and went back to his original research. Later on, Florey and Chain decided to investigate penicillin and developed ways to mass produce it but they needed to get funding. The US government were willing to fund it during the Second World War because they knew more soldiers died from infection than from their actual wounds, so penicillin would keep their soldiers alive.

Read the following feedback.

> Although this answer includes all the right information, the only **reason** it specifically identifies why penicillin took so long to be developed is that Fleming found it difficult to produce in large quantities.

To be a Level 3 answer, Answer A would need to identify and explain the reasons why penicillin wasn't mass produced. Answer B below identifies three of these reasons.

2. Use the information in Answer A to complete these sentences.

Answer B

Fleming discovered penicillin by chance but it was not part of his research work. Therefore, after he investigated it, he ....

....

....

Another reason why Fleming did not continue working on penicillin after 1928 was because he did not think it was a major breakthrough in medicine. He thought it could only be used to fight infection on the skin because ....

....

....

....

It also needed technology and funding to mass produce penicillin but Fleming didn't have this and Florey and Chain only managed to get funding in 1940 because ....

....

....

....

Activity

Now let's look at another question:

Why were Florey and Chain able to mass produce penicillin by 1944? (12 marks)

- The word 'why' reminds you to focus on reasons why they managed to do it, not a description of what they did.

- The date helps you to think about what details are relevant.

- The details you need to use should be about Florey and Chain and mass production of penicillin (not an explanation of why Fleming didn't mass produce penicillin).

A good answer is **planned** around the **reasons**.

3. Match up each reason below with the detail relevant to it. An answer based on this plan would have achieved Level 3.

1 .... 2 .... 3 .... 4 ....

Reason	Detail
1. Florey and Chain knew that penicillin was an antibiotic.	A. The government was willing to fund mass production of penicillin as they knew it would save soldiers' lives.
2. Florey and Chain set up a team of specialists.	B. They had read the article by Fleming about his investigation into penicillin.
3. They asked the American government for help.	C. Scientists at the Pfizer chemical company in New York found that freeze-drying the mould was the best way to purify it.
4. They got help in finding the most effective technology to mass produce penicillin.	D. The specialists could approach problems from different angles and share their ideas.

1B Crime and Punishment

Unit 1 is a Development Study. Questions on causation in this unit ask why change happened but also why change didn't happen (why there was continuity) or why it took so long for the situation to change. For example:

Why were the laws against smuggling so difficult to enforce in the seventeenth and eighteenth centuries? (12 marks)

The following information may help you with your answer.

In 1746, customs officers seized some smuggled goods and stored them in the Customs House at Poole in Dorset. The Hawkhurst gang then attacked the Customs House during the night and got most of the goods back. They were cheered by crowds when they stopped at Fordingbridge for breakfast.

Activity

1. Read Answer A below. Underline any reasons that you can find in it which explain why the laws against smuggling were difficult to enforce. Then check your answer with the mark scheme on page 15.

Answer A

Smuggling was usually carried out at night when ships could sail close to the shore and be unloaded in the dark. There was no police force at this time and a fairly small number of customs officers who were supposed to catch the smugglers. There were lots of different bays and coves the smugglers could use, they didn't need a normal port. The smugglers would usually get the goods moved away from the shore to their hiding place within the night but even if they were spotted most people would not inform the authorities so the laws were difficult to enforce. Lots of people got goods from the smugglers — tea, brandy, silk, tobacco, etc. Smuggled goods didn't pay tax and therefore were much cheaper than buying them in the shops. It was actually quite common for the local squire or the church minister to get things from the smugglers. However, the smugglers could also be very violent and some people were afraid of them.

Read the following feedback.

Although this answer includes all the right information, the only **reason** it specifically identifies why laws against smuggling were so difficult to enforce was that people would not inform the authorities.

To be a Level 3 answer, Answer A would need to identify and explain the reasons why it was so hard to catch smugglers. Answer B below identifies three of these reasons.

2. Use the information in Answer A to complete these sentences.

Answer B

The laws against smuggling were difficult to enforce when it was so hard to catch the smugglers. This was because there were not enough customs officers to watch all the places where smugglers might operate such as ....

....

....

Customs officers did not get much support when they tried to enforce the laws since many people supported the smugglers, including important people within the community. This was because ....

....

....

....

Some people were too afraid of the smugglers to help the authorities catch them because .....

....

....

....

Activity

Now let's look at another question:

> Why were social crimes like smuggling and poaching so difficult to deal with in the eighteenth century? (12 marks)

- The word 'why' reminds you to focus on reasons why the crimes were not dealt with, so do not give a description of the crimes.

- The date helps you to think about what details are relevant.

- The details you need to use should be about problems in dealing with these crimes (not an explanation of how the crimes were punished).

3. Match up each reason below with the detail relevant to it to create a plan for a Level 3 answer.

1 .... 2 .... 3 .... 4 ....

Reason	Detail
1. Many people felt the crimes didn't have a victim and therefore weren't real crimes.	A. They were secret activities and took place at night, in the dark.
2. It was difficult to catch someone committing these crimes.	B. They felt that poaching was done because people were hungry, while smugglers sold people goods they normally couldn't afford.
3. There was no organised police force to catch the criminals.	C. Smuggling and poaching didn't directly hurt anyone. They just meant the government lost some money and the landowner lost some animals.
4. Many people had sympathy for the criminals.	D. Although landowners often had gamekeepers and the customs officers were meant to catch smugglers, there were not enough of them.

In Unit 2 causation questions will often focus on why people did certain things or the reasons for something happening. These questions often begin with the word 'why'. For example:

> Why did white settlers often find it difficult to understand the culture of the Plains Indians? (12 marks)
>
> You may use the following in your answer and any other information of your own.
>
> • Older Plains Indians were sometimes left behind when their tribes moved on.
>
> • The Plains Indians believed in Waken Tanka.
>
> • White settlers believed land could be bought and sold.

Below is the mark scheme for Level 2 and Level 3 answers to this question.

Level	Mark	Answer
2	5–8	Student gives a **narrative or descriptive answer** about the culture of the Plains Indians.
3	9–12	Student **explains reasons why** white settlers often found it difficult to understand the culture of the Plains Indians.

Hint

A narrative or descriptive answer means you are writing 'all I know about the Plains Indians' or 'what the white settlers thought of the Plains Indians'.

Hint

Explains reasons why means you are giving reasons why you think this. You will probably use words such as 'so', 'therefore', and 'this meant that.'

Activity

1. Read Answer A below. What level would you give it and why?

Answer A

The Plains Indians were very different from the white settlers for many reasons. The first reason was due to what they wore. They normally wore clothes made from animal skins. They also lived in tipis, which were made from wood and animal skin. These were easy to build and take down. Third, the Plains Indians had their own ways of life. The Indians just left old people to die. Indian men could have as many wives as they wanted. Also there was the fact that they had various dances and ceremonies which allowed them to talk to the gods. Finally, they moved a lot as they followed the buffalo. They relied on the buffalo for everything from clothing to food to building their houses.

This answer is a Level .... because ....

....

....

2. Now complete the sentences below to explain reasons why, rather than simply describing.

The white settlers often found it hard to understand the culture of the Plains Indians because the Indians had many different beliefs.

The white settlers thought that many of their beliefs were strange such as

....

....

The Plains Indians were also nomadic which meant that they had a different lifestyle from the white settlers, for example ....

....

....

They also had different beliefs on land and so ....

....

....

The white settlers also did not understand the Plains Indians such as beliefs about warfare, which the white settlers thought ....

....

....

Activity

3. Now use the same material to write a response which focuses on a different question on the same topic. Answer the following questions on a separate sheet of paper.

> Why did many white settlers view the Plains Indians as savage? (12 marks)
>
> - Older Plains Indians were sometimes left behind when their tribes moved on.
> - The Plains Indians used the Sun Dance for help from the spirit world.
> - Plains Indians often scalped dead enemies.

4. When you have written your answer, self-assess or peer-assess it using the mark scheme on page 20.

2C Life in Germany

In Unit 2 causation questions will often focus on why people did certain things or the reasons for something happening. These questions often begin with the word 'why'. For example:

> Why were the Nazis able to persecute the Jews in Germany in the years 1933 to 1939? (12 marks)
>
> You may use the following in your answer and any other information of your own.
>
> ○ 1935: The Nuremberg Laws were passed.
>
> ○ Goebbels' Ministry of Propaganda gave daily orders to newspapers on what they could write.
>
> ○ Nazi block wardens reported people who broke the law.

Below is the mark scheme for Level 2 and Level 3 answers to this question.

Level	Mark	Answer
2	5–8	Student gives **a narrative or descriptive answer** of the Nazis' persecution of the Jews in Germany *e.g. details of Nazi treatment of the Jews 1933–39; description of propaganda.*
3	9–12	Student **explains reasons why** the Nazis were able to persecute the Jews in Germany *e.g. Nazi ideology to create a pure race; ideology of 'subhumans' and 'anti-socials'; use of SS and secret police; informers; the role of propaganda.*

Hint

A **narrative or descriptive answer** means you are writing 'all I know about the Nazis' treatment of the Jews' or 'what happened to the Jews in Germany'.

Hint

Explains reasons why means that you are giving reasons why you think this. You will probably use words such as 'so', 'therefore', and 'this meant that'.

Activity

1. Read Answer A below. What level would you give it and why?

Answer A

The Nazis persecuted the Jews in Germany first of all with the shop boycott soon after Hitler became Chancellor. Then the Nuremberg Laws were passed and marriages between pure Germans and Jews was stopped. In 1938 many of their homes and businesses were smashed up and some were sent to concentration camps. They also stopped Jews using some public places and also Jewish children were sent out of schools. Many also lost their jobs. The SS also arrested people and ordinary Germans would be breaking the law if they helped the Jews.

This answer is a Level .... because ....

....

....

2. Now complete the sentences below to explain reasons why, rather than simply describing.

The Nazis were able to persecute the Jews for many reasons. The Nuremberg Laws meant that German Jews were no longer German citizens. Therefore ....

....

....

The laws about marriage meant that Jewish children were expelled from schools so

....

....

During Kristallnacht synagogues and businesses were destroyed. So ....

....

....

The Nazis also had SS units which meant that ....

....

....

The block wardens reported people so ....

....

Activity

3. Now use the same material to write a response that focuses on a different question on the same topic. Answer the following question on a separate sheet of paper.

> Why did the lives of German Jews become so much more difficult in the years 1933 to 1939? (12 marks)
>
> You may use the following in your answer and any other information of your own.
>
> - In 1933 there was a boycott of Jewish shops.
> - Goebbels' Ministry of Propaganda gave daily orders to newspapers on what they could write.
> - In November 1938 many Jewish shops were attacked.

4. When you have written your answer, self-assess or peer-assess it using the mark scheme on page 22.

Consequence questions

When you are asked about consequences in history you should be thinking about the EFFECTS or RESULTS of something. For example:

- who was affected?   - what changed?   - how much did things change?

You also need to understand that questions asking about the importance or impact of a person or event are really consequence questions. These questions are asking how the situation changed and/or what difference the person or event made.

How do I answer consequence questions?

We can analyse consequence in history in much the same way as we analyse causation by:

- grouping the consequences into categories such as political, social, economic or religious consequences

- dividing them into short- and long-term consequences.

In other words...

Think about the effects (consequences) of a natural disaster such as a flood or earthquake. You could group the effects as:

- physical – the actual destruction of buildings, roads, etc.

- social – people forced to move from their homes, communities and families split up

- economic – trade and industry disrupted, meaning that the country makes less profit.

Or as:

- short-term effects which last for up to a year or so, such as shortage of food or clean water

- long-term effects which last for much longer, such as rebuilding large numbers of buildings.

How will I be marked?

Question 2 and questions 5(a) and 6(a) are worth 9 marks.

Questions 3 and 4 are worth 12 marks.

However, these consequence questions are all marked in the same way, using levels, going from Level 1 up to Level 3.

A 12-mark question will usually cover a broader topic than a 9-mark question, so you would be expected to write a slightly longer answer with a wider range of details for a 12-mark question. The best answers do the following things.

- Focus on EXPLANATION not description. Rather than describing what happened after an event or someone's work, you need to show how the later situation is **linked to**, or is a **consequence** of, that event or work.

- Organise your answer by classifying the consequences in some way.

- Show a range of consequences. You should aim for three or four distinct points. Depending on the question, this could mean three or four examples of economic consequences, or one example each of the economic, social and political effects.

1A Medicine and treatment

In Unit 1, questions on the effects or consequences of something will often ask you to link the consequences to a specific aspect of medicine.

Activity

1. Read the question and the table below. Different sections of the question have been colour-coded. Match up the colour-coded sections with the explanation.

Question: Explain the importance of the development of the printing press in the fifteenth century and its effect on medical knowledge and understanding. (12 marks)

1 .... 2 .... 3 .... 4 ....

Section of question	What it means in this question
1. Question command term: this tells you what sort of question it is and therefore what sort of approach you need to take in your answer.	A. The question is focused on the effects of the printing press on medical knowledge and understanding (so details of treatment are not relevant here).
2. This tells you the topic and therefore what sort of details you need to include.	B. The fifteenth century was the Renaissance period.
3. This tells you the time frame.	C. 'Explain the importance' means write about the effects this had and why they were important – what difference did this make?
4. This tells you what the focus of the question is.	D. The topic is the development of the printing press; comments about any other developments in the same time period, such as the microscope, wouldn't get any marks.

2. Read the six points in the table below. Put a tick or cross next to each one to show whether or not it is relevant to this question.

Point	Relevant?
1. Galen's ideas about treatment were based on bloodletting, purging and the Theory of Opposites.	
2. The accurate drawings of anatomy in *The Fabric of the Human Body*, published in 1543 by Vesalius, meant that doctors who had never seen a dissection done properly gained a better understanding of the human body.	
3. William Harvey published his book in 1628 explaining how the heart pumped blood around the body.	
4. Copies of Galen's books could now be produced quickly and cheaply instead of waiting for manuscript copies to be made.	
5. When something was published, everyone could read an accurate copy; there was no confusion caused by mistakes in copying.	
6. The microscope was developed during the seventeenth century.	

Now read Answer A and the feedback below.

Answer A

The printing press was a way of producing lots of copies of a document or picture very quickly and cheaply. Before this, every copy had to be written out by hand. This would take a long time and it could be expensive but also there was a risk of mistakes. Using the printing press meant every copy was the same and because hundreds of copies could be made very quickly, ideas could spread very quickly.

> This answer makes some very good points about the way that the printing press was an improvement over manuscripts. It is also about the correct time frame – BUT it is only low Level 2 because this is not linked to improvements in medicine.

This extract from the mark scheme shows the criteria for Level 2 and Level 3 answers.

| Level 2 | Answer provides information about the printing press OR about medical knowledge and understanding during the Renaissance period. |
| Level 3 | Answer shows the **effects** of the printing press on medical knowledge AND explains why they were important. |

3. Use the ideas in Answer A and the mark scheme details to demonstrate how the printing press improved medical knowledge and understanding.

When Vesalius dissected corpses, he used an artist to draw the muscles, nerves and skeleton. These were printed in his book 'The Fabric of the Human Body' which was published in 1543. These drawings showed the structure of the body very accurately. This helped doctors because

....

....

The fact that Harvey's book included diagrams of his experiments encouraged other doctors to think about whether Galen's ideas were right. This was important because ....

....

....

Once these new ideas had been accepted, doctors realised that Galen was not always right and medical training began to change. It was easy for doctors to keep up with new ideas because

....

....

Hint

A 12-mark question could also ask: '**How important was** the printing press in the development of medicine?'

A Level 3 answer to this question would need to show there were both positive and negative consequences: for example, improved knowledge of the structure of the body did not actually change doctors' ideas about disease, so the printing press had very little effect on understanding **disease** or on the treatments used.

In Unit 1, questions on the effects or consequences of something will often ask you to link the consequences to a specific aspect of crime and punishment.

Activity

1. Read the question and the table below. Different sections of the question have been colour-coded. Match up the colour-coded sections with the explanation.

> Why was Elizabeth Fry important in changing attitudes towards punishment during the nineteenth century? (12 marks)

1 .... 2 .... 3 .... 4 ....

Section of question	What it means in this question
1. Question command term: this tells you what sort of question it is and therefore what sort of approach you need to take in your answer.	A. The question specifies changing attitudes towards punishment, so the focus should be on this, not on descriptions of punishment.
2. This tells you the topic and therefore what sort of detail you need to include.	B. The nineteenth century was the 1800s.
3. This tells you what the focus of the question is.	C. The topic is Elizabeth Fry; comments about the work of John Howard won't get any marks unless they are linked to Fry.
4. This tells you the time frame.	D. 'Why was she important' means write about the effects of what she did. What difference did she make?

2. Read the five points in the table below. Put a tick or cross next to each one to show whether or not it is relevant to this question.

Point	Relevant?
1. Elizabeth Fry visited female prisoners in Newgate Gaol, London, and took in clean straw and clothes for the women, saying that if they were treated like decent people they would behave better.	
2. She said that if the women had a way to earn money while in prison and after their release, they would be less likely to go back to a life of crime. She was inspired by her Quaker religion.	
3. If the prisons were full, prisoners were sometimes kept on old sailing ships called 'hulks'.	
4. She campaigned for change by writing a book to publicise the conditions in prison, set up a school in the prison for the women and children, started a Ladies' Association to visit the prisoners and gave evidence to parliament about what changes needed to be made.	
5. Many of the reforms she suggested were included in Robert Peel's Gaol Act in 1823.	

Now read Answer A and the feedback below.

Answer A

Elizabeth Fry suggested that treating prisoners decently and teaching them about religion would make them more likely to be truly sorry for their crimes. She also said that teaching the women some kind of trade would make them less likely to go back to crime. These ideas were important because they fitted in with the ideas of other reformers about the value of human life and that punishment should not just be about revenge but should try to reform the prisoner and rehabilitate them into society.

This answer makes some very good points about what Fry did, and her ideas about punishment. It is also about the correct time frame – BUT it is only Level 2 because it doesn't show what effect her work had.

This extract from the mark scheme shows the criteria for Level 2 and Level 3 answers.

| Level 2 | Answer provides information about attitudes towards punishment OR about the work of Fry. |
| Level 3 | Answer shows the **effects** of the work of Fry on attitudes towards punishment AND explains why they were important. |

3. Use the ideas in Answer A and the mark scheme details to demonstrate how her work influenced other people.

Elizabeth Fry wanted prison to reform the criminals instead of just punishing them.

She suggested that ....

....

Other people found out about her ideas through ....

....

When the 1823 Gaols Act introduced female warders for female prisoners and regular

visits from a chaplain, it showed that Fry's ideas ....

....

....

Hint

If the question had asked '**How important** was the work of Elizabeth Fry', the answer could also have pointed out that the idea of reform continued in the separate system later in the century but there was also a change back to the idea of revenge and hard labour in the silent system, so her ideas only had a limited impact.

2B The American West

Questions dealing with consequences will often expect you to show how events changed people's lives in different ways. For example:

> Describe the effects of the discovery of gold in California in 1848 on the settlement of the American West (9 marks).

Hint

A narrative or descriptive answer means you are simply 'telling the story' of the discovery of gold in California in 1848.

Level	Mark	
2	4–6	Student **describes or narrates the discovery of gold** in California in 1848.
3	7–9	Student **explains the effects** of the discovery of gold in California in 1848 on the settlement of the American West.

Hint

Explain the effects means that you show a number of different effects such as:
a. political, social, economic effects
b. effects on different groups of people.

Activity

First, let's look at some of the effects of the discovery of gold in California in 1848.

1. Read statements A–J in the table below. Decide whether each statement DESCRIBES (Level 2) or EXPLAINS (Level 3) the effects, and put a tick in the appropriate column.

	Statement	Level 2	Level 3
A	60 ships left ports in America and in Europe.		
B	The mining towns were poor and there was disease.		
C	This led to the development of the Californian economy and the growth of San Francisco.		
D	The men had the nickname the 'forty-niners'.		
E	After the gold near the surface had been mined, many left.		
F	Foreign miners had to pay taxes.		
G	Some men made vast fortunes but the majority eventually returned home.		
H	Crimes such as 'claim-jumping' developed due to the lack of law enforcement.		
I	Further discoveries of gold from 1858 encouraged further migration.		
J	There were nearly 600 saloons in San Francisco by the 1860s.		

2. Have a go at answering the question using the writing frame on page 30. Aim to write an answer which shows a RANGE OF EFFECTS of the discovery of gold in 1848. You can use the information from the table above to help.

The discovery of gold in California in 1848 had several effects on the development of the American West. Some benefitted such as .... but for others it ....

....

The rapid development of mining towns lead to problems such as ....

....

....

....

But there were also some benefits to the USA such as ....

....

....

Now check your answer using the following checklist.

Have you included at least THREE different groups of people?	
Have you shown groups which benefitted from the gold rush?	
Have you explained why these groups of people benefitted?	
Have you shown groups which did not benefit from the gold rush?	
Have you explained why these groups of people did not benefit?	

Activity

Let's look at another 'consequences' question.

Describe the effects of the discovery of gold in the Black Hills, Dakota, in 1874 on the settlement of the American West. (9 marks)

3. Write five statements that EXPLAIN a RANGE of the effects of this discovery of gold which together will make a Level 3 answer. Remember you can also show a RANGE of effects in your answer by covering different groups of people.

1	
2	
3	
4	
5	

Questions dealing with consequences will often expect you to show how events changed people's lives in different ways. For example:

> Describe the effects of hyperinflation in 1923 on Germany. (9 marks)

Hint

A narrative or descriptive answer means you are simply 'telling the story' of what happened in Germany during the hyperinflation of 1923.

Level	Mark	
2	4–6	Student **describes or narrates** events of 1923.
3	7–9	Student explains a **range of effects** of hyperinflation

Hint

A range of effects means you show a number of different effects of hyperinflation, such as:

a. political, social, economic effects

b. effects on different groups of people.

Activity

First, let's look at some of the effects of hyperinflation in Germany in 1923.

1. Read statements A–J in the table below. Decide whether each statement DESCRIBES (Level 2) or EXPLAINS (Level 3) the effects, and put a tick in the appropriate column.

	Statement	Level 2	Level 3
A	Banknotes were so worthless people used them to light fires with. Children played with money as well.		
B	Old people suffered a lot because their pensions became worthless but those people in debt benefitted because their debts were wiped out.		
C	The hyperinflation had political consequences as many Germans resented the Weimar government more.		
D	Hyperinflation is when prices go up very quickly. This happened in Germany in 1923.		
E	A man went into a shop and in between ordering a coffee and paying for it, the coffee had become twice as expensive.		
F	Some farmers benefitted during the hyperinflation because food prices went up.		
G	The German government had to print more money to pay for reparations.		
H	Richer Germans did not suffer as much because they often owned land.		
I	Many middle-class Germans particularly resented inflation because their savings were wiped out.		
J	A loaf of bread cost 70,000 marks in the summer of 1923.		

2. Have a go at answering the question using the writing frame below. Aim to write an answer which will show A RANGE OF EFFECTS of hyperinflation on Germany in 1923. You can use the information from the table on page 31 to help you.

In 1923 hyperinflation affected people in Germany in many different ways. For some people it made things very difficult. People such as .... and .... suffered a lot because ....

....

Other people did well such as ....

....

because ....

....

It made the situation difficult for the Weimar government because ....

....

Now check your answers using the checklist below.

Have you included at least THREE different groups of people?	
Have you shown the groups that suffered during the hyperinflation?	
Have you explained why these groups of people suffered?	
Have you shown groups that did well during the hyperinflation?	
Have you explained why these groups of people did well?	

Activity

Let's look at another 'consequences' question.

> Describe the effects of the Reichstag Fire in February 1933 on Hitler's rise to power (9 marks).

3. Write five statements that EXPLAIN a RANGE of the effects of the Reichstag Fire on Hitler's rise to power which together will make a Level 3 answer. Remember you can also show a RANGE of effects in your answer by covering different groups of people.

1	
2	
3	
4	
5	

Role questions

In history we often try to see what effect a person or a factor has had on a situation. This is often called the role of an individual or the role of a factor.

How do I answer role questions?

When you answer a role question or a question asking how important a person was, you need to explain how that person or factor affected other aspects of the situation. Explain whether the person or factor had a positive or negative influence. Was the role to act as a catalyst and speed up the process of change, or as a hindrance, slowing it down?

How will I be marked?

Question 2 and questions 5(a) and 6(a) are worth 9 marks. Questions 3 and 4 are worth 12 marks.

However, they are all marked in the same way, using levels from Level 1 up to Level 3.

Level	Answer
2	At this level the answer **provides information** about the person or factor, e.g. **describes** what happened or what the person did, or describes the situation before/after.
3	Level 3 answers can explain why the role of the person or factor was **positive/negative** or how it affected other factors involved in the situation.

Make sure you focus on EXPLANATION not description when writing your answers.

So, rather than describing what happened or writing about events that involved the person or factor, you need to show how the person or factor fitted into the overall situation and what sort of effect the person or factor had.

In other words...

Neil Armstrong could not have been the first man to set foot on the moon without developments in science and technology – that **factor** was **essential**. However, **his role as an individual** was **not essential** – the moon walk could still have happened without him because other astronauts were trained to do it as well.

The role of an individual like the head teacher, will depend on their personal qualities. Other people could do the same job but they would do it in a different way and possibly the results would be different. Head teachers know that a positive attitude helps to make learning effective, so one head might focus on rewarding students' achievements, whereas another might prefer to visit lessons to focus on students' attitudes in the learning environment.

The type of question about the role of an individual or factor that you will get in Unit 1 (Medicine or Crime) is shown on pages 34–37 and the type that you will get in Unit 2 (The American West or Life in Germany) is shown on pages 38–41.

1A Medicine and treatment

In Unit 1, questions can be set on certain **key people** who are named in the specification. Therefore you **MUST** know about: Galen, Vesalius, William Harvey, Edward Jenner, Louis Pasteur, Robert Koch, Florence Nightingale, Elizabeth Garrett Anderson, Alexander Fleming, and Crick and Watson.

- If you are doing Extension Study 1, you also need to know about Hippocrates.
- If you are doing Extension Study 2, you also need to know about Edwin Chadwick, John Snow and Aneurin Bevan.

The factors that are most often discussed in medicine are: religion, chance (luck), individuals, war, government, science, technology and social beliefs. However, there are other possibilities, such as education, medical training or communication.

Here is an example of a Unit 1 question that looks at the role of a factor.

> Why have science and technology been so important in improving medical understanding since 1850? (12 marks)
>
> You may use the following in your answer and any other information of your own.
> - Louis Pasteur published his Germ Theory in 1861.
> - X-rays were discovered in 1895.
> - Crick and Watson discovered the structure of DNA in 1953.

Activity

1. Study Answer A, then use the checklist below to decide what Level it is.

Answer A

Science and technology have been very important in improving medical understanding since 1850. This is because Louis Pasteur published his Germ Theory in 1861 which helped people to understand about germs. He carried out experiments with liquid in an open flask and another flask where he bent the neck of the flask and put water into the bend. This prevented air from reaching the liquid in the flask. This shows how science helped medicine.

An example of technology helping medicine is when Roentgen discovered X-rays. Hospitals could use X-ray machines to find whether someone's bone was broken or where bullets were inside the body. We also have other technology like ultrasound scans and CAT scans.

Crick and Watson discovered the structure of DNA in 1953. This was very important because lots of conditions are the result of genetic problems.

Level 2	✓	Level 3	✓
Describes an aspect of Pasteur's Germ Theory.		Explains how Pasteur's Germ Theory changed people's ideas about what caused illness.	
Shows that X-rays began to be used in medicine.		Explains how X-rays made a difference to medical understanding.	
Shows that understanding DNA is linked to medicine.		Explains how an improved understanding of DNA changed our understanding of illness.	
Describes examples of science and technology linked to medicine.		Uses examples of science and technology to show how medical understanding changed.	

Overall level ....

2. Now have a go at writing an improved answer to this question using the writing frame below. Use the same details but make sure you show how each example **improved** medical **understanding** (not simply medical treatment).

When Louis Pasteur published his Germ Theory in 1861 it proved that disease was not spread by miasma or by spontaneous generation. This meant people now began to identify the microbes which caused disease, which was important because ....
....

TB shows up like a shadow on the lungs in an X-ray and other examples of technology helping doctors to find out what is wrong are ....
....

Some conditions are not an illness that you catch but a genetic problem that is inherited, for example cystic fibrosis. Once we understand how these are caused, scientists can then work on treating and preventing them, so it was a big step forwards when ....
....

Activity

3 Read the following question and look for the key parts in it.

> How important was the role of Elizabeth Garrett Anderson in improving the position of women within medicine in the late nineteenth century? (12 marks)

You should have spotted **the topic** (Elizabeth Garrett Anderson), **time frame** (late nineteenth century, which is 1850–1900), **command term** (how important – what difference she made) and **focus** (improving the position of women in medicine).

4. Now plan an answer to this question by matching up each point with the relevant example.

1 .... 2 .... 3 .... 4 .... 5 ....

Point	Example
1. It was difficult for a woman to become a qualified doctor.	A. Students signed a petition to prevent her from joining their lectures and dissections; she had to pay for private sessions.
2. Elizabeth Garrett Anderson faced opposition when she wanted to train as a doctor.	B. The Society of Apothecaries changed its regulations so that no other women could qualify as a doctor in the same way.
3. Elizabeth Garrett Anderson registered as a doctor in 1865.	C. The government passed an Act allowing women to qualify as doctors in 1876.
4. The position of women in medicine changed very little in the short term.	D. Doctors were expected to have had training at a university or medical school but these would not admit women students.
5. The problem was only solved when the government took action.	E. When she passed the exams set by the Society of Apothecaries, they would not register her as qualified until her father took them to court.

1B Crime and punishment

Questions can be set on certain **key people** who are named in the specification. Therefore you MUST know about: Guy Fawkes, Jonathan Wild, the Fielding brothers, Sir Robert Peel, John Howard, Elizabeth Fry and Derek Bentley.

The **factors** that are most often discussed in crime and punishment are: religion, individuals, economic and social conditions, government, science and technology, and social beliefs. However, there are other possibilities, such as the role of the media.

Here is an example of a Unit 1 question that asks you to consider the role of a factor.

> Why has technology been such an important factor affecting crime and policing since 1900? (12 marks)
>
> You may use the following in your answer and any other information of your own.
>
> - In 1935 the police Forensic Science Laboratory was set up.
> - In 1939, 25 per cent of all crime involved motoring offences.
> - In 2001 the government set up the National High Tech Crime Squad to deal with computer crime.

Activity

1. Study Answer A, and then use the checklist to decide what Level it is.

Answer A

Technology has played an important role in both crime and policing since 1900. New examples of old crimes have been committed such as theft of a car or criminals using a car to get away from the crime scene. However, there are also new types of crimes like drink-driving, not having a licence and speeding. Other new crimes have involved computers, for example, identity theft, computer hacking or sending a virus. Another example of technology is terrorism. Bombs can be set off by remote control or by using timers.

Technology has also been important for the police. Special squads have been set up to deal with car crime or with computer crime. The police also use computers to check fingerprints and keep records of individual criminals. Tracking systems linked to computers also help the police to track down criminals. The phone has been an important way for the police to communicate and also for the public to report a crime or to ask for help when they need it.

Level 2	✓	Level 3	✓
Describes an aspect of technology which is linked to existing crime.		Explains how technology is used to commit existing crime.	
Describes an aspect of technology which is linked to new crimes.		Explains how technology is used to commit new crimes.	
Describes an aspect of technology which is linked to existing methods of policing.		Explains how technology is used in existing methods of policing.	
Describes an aspect of technology which is linked to new aspects of policing.		Explains how technology is used in new aspects of policing.	

Overall level ....

2. Write an improved answer to this question. Use the same details but make sure it shows how each example **changed** the existing situation. Starter sentences have been provided for you.

Developments in technology have helped the criminal because machines such as the car or computer mean there are more or 'better' ways to commit crimes. For example, theft is easier to commit because ....
....

However, developments in technology have also created new crimes which didn't exist before. For example, ...
....

Developments in technology have had similar effects on the police. Some things which they already did have become much easier. For example, keeping records about crimes and criminals, proving who committed a crime or chasing criminals have all changed because
....

New technology has also brought in some new areas of work for the police, such as
....

Activity

3. Read through the following question and look for the key parts in it.

> How important was the role of the Fielding brothers in improving law and order in the late eighteenth century? (12 marks)

You should have spotted **the topic** (role of the Fielding brothers), **time frame** (late eighteenth century, which is 1750–1800), **command term** (how important – what difference did they make) and **focus** (improving law and order).

4. Now plan an answer to this question by matching up each point with the relevant example.

1 .... 2 .... 3 .... 4 .... 5 ....

Point	Example
1. Henry Fielding was a magistrate at Bow Street, London, who wanted to reduce crime.	A. In 1829, Robert Peel set up the Metropolitan Police Force.
2. In 1754 John Fielding set up the Bow Street Horse patrols.	B. Henry printed information about crimes and criminals in the *Covent Garden Journal*.
3. Henry Fielding thought that sharing information about crime and criminals would reduce crime.	C. The amount of highway robbery was reduced in 1763 when the government paid for patrols on the main routes into London.
4. Sir John Fielding suggested that the idea of the Bow Street Runners should be extended to cover the whole London area.	D. Patrols by Runners on horseback reduced crimes in that area because criminals knew there was an increased risk of being caught.
5. The work of the Fieldings showed how important it was to have a well organised force available to detect and prevent crime.	E. In 1749 he set up a small group called the Bow Street Runners to track down criminals and recover stolen property.

2B The American West

In Unit 2 there are sometimes questions that ask you to explain the role of an individual or group or a factor. This means looking at the impact they had on events in the past. For example:

> Describe the contribution made by women to the white settlement of the Plains. (9 marks).

Activity

1. Read Answer A. Underline the information that is **not** relevant for this question.

Answer A

There were lots of problems facing the early homesteaders. The weather was often severe and it was difficult to farm the land. The lack of water meant that it was difficult to farm the land. There were other hazards such as plagues of grasshoppers. Fires also damaged their farm land. But in many ways women helped the white settlement of the Plains. Women did a lot of work. They looked after the needs of the family. They collected chips for fuel and made fires, cooked and made sure the home was heated. They looked after smaller animals and some of the crops. They also helped to build houses. Women also looked after children. They made clothes, cooked food and made sure the family was cared for properly. Some women also worked as teachers and there was a campaign to get more female teachers. They made sure the children were cared for. Women often collected water from wells or rivers. Women were therefore important to the white settlement of the Plains.

This would be a Level 2 answer. It describes women homesteaders, but it does not describe their **contribution** to the white settlement of the Plains.

2. Now write an improved answer to the same question using at least THREE of the following specific details provided below.

Wyoming Territory	Disease	Childbirth	Recruitment of teachers	Sod-houses

....

....

....

....

....

....

....

Hint
Make sure that you describe the CONTRIBUTION (the difference made) by women to the white settlement of the Plains.

Activity

Now use the same information to answer a different question on the same topic area. Notice the dates given for this question.

> In what ways did conditions on the Plains affect the lives of women homesteaders in the 1850s and 1860s? (9 marks)

3. Put a cross by the boxes below not relevant for this particular question.

Sod-houses		Wind pumps		Building of railroads	
Disease		Education		Isolation	
Mass-produced machinery		Turkey Red wheat		Childbirth	

4. Now use the relevant information to write your answer.

....

....

....

....

....

....

....

....

....

....

....

....

Activity

Here is another question on the role of a group:

> Describe the part played by cattle ranchers in the Johnson County War in 1892. (9 marks)

5. On a separate piece of paper write an answer to this question that clearly focuses on the role played by cattle ranchers in the Johnson County War. Make sure you include some specific details.

2C Life in Germany

In Unit 2 there are sometimes questions that ask you to explain the role of an individual, a group or a factor. This means looking at the impact they had on events in the past. For example:

> Describe the importance of the work of Goebbels as Minister of Enlightenment and Propaganda. (9 marks)

Activity

1. Read Answer A. Underline any information **not** relevant for this question.

Answer A

In the very early years of the Nazi Party Goebbels had even been a threat to Hitler's leadership. After the Beer Hall Putsch Hitler decided that the Nazis were going to use different methods to get into power. They were not going to use force but now they decided they would need votes to get into power. Goebbels was one of Hitler's earliest and most loyal supporters. Goebbels job was to make sure the Nazis got their message across with specific messages for different groups of people such as farmers, workers and women. Goebbels was in charge of what could be published. There were mass rallies and marches which demonstrated the organised and powerful Nazi government. People could listen to Hitler's speeches on cheap mass-produced radios. There were new developments in technology, and films like 'The Eternal Jew' were made that carried the Nazi message. The Nazis made sure as many people as possible could hear their ideas. The use of propaganda was a factor in stopping opposition to the Nazi government.

This is a Level 2 answer. It is a description of the work of Goebbels and propaganda in Nazi Germany, but it does not describe the **importance** of his work.

2. Now write an improved answer to the same question, using at least THREE of the following specific details provided below.

Anti-Semitism	Nuremberg Rallies	Reich Chamber of Culture	Book-burnings	1936 Berlin Olympics

....

....

....

....

....

Hint

Make sure that you describe the IMPORTANCE (the difference made) by Goebbels and his work as Minister of Propaganda and Enlightenment.

....

....

Activity

Use the same information to answer a different question on the same topic area. Notice the dates given for this question.

> In what ways did the Nazi government use propaganda to control Germany in the years 1933 to 1939? (9 marks)

3. Put a cross by the boxes below **not** relevant for this particular question.

Wall Street Crash		Munich (Beer Hall) Putsch		Nuremberg Rallies	
Berlin Olympics		'The Eternal Jew'		Images of Hitler	
Reich Chamber of Culture		Radios		Hitler Youth military units	

4. Now use the relevant information to write your answer.

....

....

....

....

....

....

....

....

....

....

....

Activity

Here is another question on the role of an individual.

> Describe the role of Pastor Niemöller in opposing the Nazi government. (9 marks)

5. On a separate piece of paper write an answer to this question that clearly focuses on Pastor Niemöller's role in opposing the Nazi government. Make sure you include some specific details.

Analysis and evaluation questions

When you analyse something you break it down into key sections or points so that they can each be looked at separately. You have already seen this in questions about the causes or consequences of an event, or about the role or significance of a specific person or factor. Each time you identify different reasons or effects, or different factors, you are **analysing** the situation.

This is also the skill involved when a question asks 'in what ways...' or if questions 5(a) and 6(a) ask you to describe the key features of a topic. To answer these questions well, you should group the information in some way rather than just list everything you can think of.

In other words...

Someone talking about you might mention how well you are doing at school, your taste in music, the fact that you are the eldest child in the family and the fact that you love a particular football team. These points could be grouped together, using headings such as family, school and leisure interests.

How will I be marked?

Questions 5(a) and 6(a) are worth 9 marks; questions 3 and 4 are worth 12 marks. The best answers include a range of different aspects (at least three) and explain how they have been grouped.

Level	Answer
1	Answer offers a simple or general answer, supported by very little detail.
2	Answer offers a list of examples or explains one example in depth.
3	Answer shows a range of different aspects, explaining how they have been grouped.

For example: if a question asked about the key features of medical treatment in the Middle Ages, an answer explaining bleeding and purging would be Level 2 because these are both treatments based on the Four Humours. A Level 3 answer would include other types of treatment, such as prayer and charms, based on supernatural ideas, and herbal remedies, based on practical experience.

In a question asking in what ways law enforcement changed in the period 1450–1900, you would be expected to write about the hue and cry, local constables and watchmen, the Bow Street Runners and the police force. However, the best answers would explain the shift from community-based law enforcement by unpaid officials to a professional organisation.

If the question asked about the key features of the lives of American Plains Indians, the best answers would organise information to cover spiritual beliefs, the social structure of the tribe, the nomadic lifestyle following the buffalo, and beliefs about warfare. In an answer to a question asking in what ways the Nazis used education, information could be grouped to cover indoctrination of boys and girls with ideas about their role in society, the spread of Nazi ideas, such as anti-Semitism and a belief in Hitler as a great leader.

However, some questions go further – they ask you to **evaluate** two or more aspects. These evaluation questions can ask you:

- about the most important cause or the most important consequence
- to compare two different people or periods and say which was most important
- to compare two different periods and say how similar or how different they were
- to identify aspects of change and aspects of continuity within a period and say which was more important.

How do I answer evaluation questions?

First you need to identify the various causes or consequences, or examples of change and continuity or similarity and difference. You should also be able to provide details to support your comments.

You then need to evaluate or weigh up the different aspects. For example, there might be great similarity in ideas, but differences in what action was taken. There might be great change for a few people but continuity for the majority of society. One factor might be important in the short term and another factor more important in the long term.

In other words...

What is the most important reason why you like your best friend? Is it the fact that you've known each other for a long time? Is it a shared interest in a sport or shared taste in music? Or do you share the same sense of humour and attitude towards life? You have to think about all the reasons you are friends before you can say which is the most important reason.

How similar are you and your best friend? You might share the same sense of humour or attitude to life, but perhaps one of you is more 'sporty' and the other is more 'creative' in your leisure interests – is that a big difference? Does it mean that actually you're not very similar overall? Or are you very similar, despite this small area of difference?

Questions 5(b) and 6(b) will always have three bullet points designed to give you some ideas about the different sorts of argument that you could use in your answer.

For example, if you are asked to compare two different people or periods, there will be at least one bullet point about each of them – this reminds you that your answer should include both of them.

If you are asked about which factor or event was most important, at least one bullet point will be about the factor named in the question but at least one bullet point will be about something different, in order to remind you to think about other possibilities.

There is no 'right' answer to these questions. You just need to make sure you focus on what the question is asking.

- If it is about comparing importance, make sure you say why each aspect was important.
- If it is about similarity or difference, make sure you point out which bits are similar and which bits are different.
- If it is about change or continuity, point out examples of change and examples of continuity.

Question types: orange, iceberg or scales?

- An 'orange' question is one where you need to separate out the different segments. Questions that begin 'why' or 'what were the causes/effects' are orange questions. Here your answer should have three or four sections, each dealing with a different cause or consequence. Questions that ask 'what were the key features' are also 'orange' questions.

- Only the tip of an iceberg actually sticks up out of the water – 9/10 of the iceberg is out of sight. An 'iceberg' question mentions one reason or effect and asks if that was the most important, but your answer needs to talk about the 'hidden' other reasons or effects as well as the one mentioned in the question.

- A 'scales' question is one which begins 'how far' or 'to what extent'. Your essay will divide into three sections: the first section will give details that agree with the statement and your second section will be where you give details that disagree with the statement – just like balancing the two sides of a pair of scales. But very often the two sides are not equally heavy and the third section of your essay weighs up the evidence on each side of the issue in order to answer the question. Questions that ask things like 'how much change' are also 'scales' questions. They are asking you to say which side of the scales is heaviest but only one side has been mentioned in the question. If you are asked 'How much change was there in the period?' you have to talk about continuity as well before you can decide how big the changes were.

How will I be marked?

These questions will often be worth 16 marks. This is because you are dealing with a range of points, analysing them to show how they were a cause or consequence or to identify change and continuity, or similarity and difference, and you are then evaluating their importance in order to make a judgement.

The mark scheme will follow the same pattern you have already seen, but there will be an additional Level 4.

Level	Marks	Descriptor
1	1–4	Answer offers a simple or general answer, supported by very little detail OR answer offers brief detail on one aspect of the question.
2	5–8	Answer offers accurate detail but does not show how this detail is relevant to this question.
3	9–12	Answer responds to the specific question, analysing details to show importance, similarity, difference, change or continuity.
4	13–16	Answer responds to the specific question, analysing details to show importance, similarity, difference, change or continuity and then evaluates them in order to reach a conclusion.

In questions 5(b)/6(b) there are also additional marks for spelling, punctuation and grammar as shown in the mark scheme on page 45.

Spelling, punctuation and grammar

In question 5(b) and 6(b) there are additional marks for spelling, punctuation and grammar: up to 3 marks in Unit 1 and up to 4 marks in Unit 2. The table below shows how you will be marked.

Unit 1 Question 5(b)/6(b)	Unit 2 Question 5(b)/6(b)	
0 marks	0 marks	Errors severely hinder the meaning of the response or students do not spell, punctuate or use the rules of grammar within the context of the demands of the question.
Level 1: Threshold performance		Students spell, punctuate and use the rules of grammar with reasonable accuracy in the context of the demands of the question. Any errors do not hinder meaning in the response. Where required, they use a limited range of specialist terms appropriately.
1 mark	1 mark	
Level 2: Intermediate performance		Students spell, punctuate and use the rules of grammar with considerable accuracy and general control of meaning in the context of the demands of the question. Where required, they use a good range of specialist terms with facility.
2 marks	2–3 marks	
Level 3: High performance		Students spell, punctuate and use the rules of grammar with consistent accuracy and effective control of meaning in the context of the demands of the question. Where required, they use a wide range of specialist terms adeptly and with precision.
3 marks	4 marks	

Planning your answer

It is vital that your answer to an evaluation question contains an 'argument'. This does not mean insisting that your ideas are correct and other ideas are wrong or stupid. It means having a clear sense of your overall answer running through the whole essay, fitting all the jigsaw pieces together into a single picture.

Good answers are well structured and build up a logical argument. A good structure for your answer would be as follows:

- Introduction: state your overall argument (which was the most important factor/how similar were the two periods /how much change was there?)

- Section 1: If something is mentioned in the question (Explain whether technology was the most important reason why …), deal with that first; if nothing is mentioned, deal with the cause or factor you think is most important. If the question is about continuity or similarity, deal first with whatever is mentioned in the question or the earlier period.

- Section 2: Deal with the alternative causes or factors, or the other side of the issue.

- Conclusion: Make your judgement, explaining your criteria clearly – how have you decided what was most important/how similar two periods were, etc. ?

Hint

Students who write good answers to evaluation questions often write a brief plan before they start writing their answer. It is a good idea to spend up to five minutes noting down headings for your different paragraphs.

1A Medicine and treatment

Unit 1 is a Development Study. Change and continuity are key themes. The 16-mark question comes in the Extension Studies (each one covers a different period, so check with your teacher which one you are studying).

- Extension Study 1 covers Medicine and public health from Roman Britain to c.1350
- Extension Study 2 covers Public health c.1350 to present day.

However, the examples used below will be based on material from the core content, Medicine and Treatment c.1350 to present day. They will therefore be relevant to you whichever Extension Study you have covered, and you can use them to practise evaluation skills and essay planning.

Activity

1. Using the information about different types of question on page 44, complete the grid below. The first one has been done for you.

Question	Type	How to answer
Why did it take so long to find vaccinations for diseases besides smallpox?	Orange	Explain how each of 3 or 4 points was a reason for the delay.
How different was medical training during the Middle Ages from medical training during the nineteenth century?		
Was chance the main reason why Jenner discovered a vaccination against smallpox?		
How much did treatment of infectious diseases change in the years c.1348–1665?		
What was the most important consequence of Pasteur's Germ Theory?		
Why did Galen's ideas stay important for so long?		

Read the question below.

> Who was more important in the development of penicillin – Fleming or Florey and Chain? (16 marks)
>
> You may use the following in your answer and any other information of your own.
>
> - 1929: Fleming published an article on penicillin.
> - 1940: Florey and Chain tested penicillin on mice.
> - 1941: Florey flew to the USA.

This is a 'scales' question. To answer this question properly you need to explain why Fleming was important, why Florey and Chain were important, and then explain your judgement about who was more important.

Answer A below has all the necessary information but it is written as a narrative account and therefore would only be a Level 2 answer.

Answer A

In the 1920s Fleming found that a mould had killed the bacteria he was growing for his research. Fleming studied this mould (penicillin) and found it was an antibiotic and he successfully used it to treat an eye infection. However, it was difficult to purify and to produce in large quantities. He found that it was killed by acid in the stomach so he felt that it would not be very useful as a medicine. Therefore, he wrote up his work in an article in 1929 and went back to his original research.

During the 1930s Florey and Chain were working on ways of fighting bacteria when Chain read Fleming's article and they decided to work on penicillin. They tested it successfully on mice in 1940 and in 1941 on humans. However, one of their patients died when supplies of penicillin ran out because they still could not produce it in large enough quantities to be effective. British companies were already working at full capacity producing existing medicines, so Florey flew to the USA where the government offered funding to mass produce penicillin.

To improve Answer A these details need to be combined with an explanation that gives the reasons why Fleming and Florey and Chain were important in the development of penicillin.

2. Match the comments with the explanations in the table below to make explained comments.

1 .... 2 .... 3 .... 4 .... 5 ....

Comment about importance	Explanation
1. Fleming was very important in the development of penicillin because he …	A. could read about his research and build on it to develop new approaches.
2. His article shared his findings with other scientists who …	B. so that it could be available for use on a large scale.
3. It was Florey and Chain who …	C. so that people realised how useful it could be in medicine.
4. They developed ways to purify it …	D. originally identified it as an antibiotic and investigated its properties.
5. They also got funding …	E. showed its effectiveness on humans.

3. Now write a conclusion explaining who you think was more important. There is no 'right' answer here – excellent answers could explain why Florey and Chain's work would not have happened without Fleming's earlier work, or for explaining that, without Florey and Chain, penicillin would never have been developed.

....

....

....

....

Read the following question and Answer B below.

> How much change was there in the understanding and treatment of illness in the period c.1500 – c.1900? (16 marks)
>
> You may use the following in your answer and any other information of your own.
>
> - 1543: Vesalius published 'The Fabric of the Human Body'.
>
> - More than 92,000 people came to be touched by King Charles II (1660–85) in an attempt to be cured of scrofula.
>
> - 1861: Pasteur's Germ Theory.

Answer B

In the period c.1500–c.1900 there were many changes in medicine. The work of Vesalius and Harvey helped to provide a better understanding of human anatomy and the fact that their work was published meant that their ideas could spread quickly and began to be taught in medical schools and universities. Then in the eighteenth century, John Hunter dissected many bodies to get an understanding of conditions such as arthritis and how a disease progressed. Therefore by 1900 there had been huge changes in the understanding of the body and how illness affected it.

However, ideas about the cause of disease remained the same for most of this period. In 1500, the main ideas about illness were that it was caused by something supernatural (God or the movement of the planets), by miasma (that illness was caused by poisonous vapours in the air) or by an imbalance of the Four Humours. Although there was less belief in supernatural causes of illness by the eighteenth century, ideas about miasma and the Four Humours were still key theories about the cause of illness throughout this period. It was not until 1861, when Pasteur showed that microbes caused illness, that there was a big change.

4. Below are three sets of marks and feedback for this question. Highlight which mark and comment you think is the correct one for Answer B.

> Top Level 2, 8 marks
> Lots of good detail about understanding and treatment of disease but little focus on change.
>
> Top Level 3, 12 marks
> Good explanation of various examples of change and continuity in this period but no judgement about 'how much' change occurred.
>
> Top Level 4, 16 marks
> Excellent examples of both change and continuity in understanding of illness and weighs up the two sides of the issue in order to make a judgement about how much change there was.

Activity

Read the following question.

How similar were the ways people responded to the plague in the Middle Ages and to cholera in the nineteenth century? (16 marks)

You may use the following in your answer and any other information of your own.

- Flagellants whipped themselves during the Black Death in 1348.
- Pest houses were set up on the edge of towns to isolate plague sufferers.
- Barrels of tar were burned in the street to purify the air during cholera epidemics.

Remember

If you are being asked to compare and reach a judgement on 'how similar', you have to look at similarities and differences before you can weigh them up and decide.

5. Colour-code the points in the table, underlining similarities in blue and differences in red.

	Plague in the Middle Ages	**Cholera in the 19th century**
Ideas about cause	Religion; imbalance of Four Humours; miasma	Imbalance of Four Humours; miasma; spontaneous generation
Treatment	Bleeding and purging; herbal remedies; trying to get the poison out of the buboes	Bleeding and purging; herbal remedies; patent medicines
Prevention	Flagellants; keeping the air moving; isolation; burning rubbish	Burning tar; burning rubbish; smoking cigars
Action by government or local authorities	Days of prayer and fasting ordered; clean up of towns ordered	Clean up of towns ordered

6. Now complete the following writing frame to write a good answer to this question.

There was a lot of similarity in the ways people responded to the plague and to cholera. For example, in both cases people would try to treat the disease by ....
....

The ways they tried to prevent themselves from catching the plague were also similar. For example, ...
....

This similarity in what they did was because they had similar ideas about the causes of disease ....
....

However, there were some differences. For example, ...
....

Now try to improve the answer by writing a conclusion that weighs up both sides and reaches a judgement on **how much** similarity there was between the reactions to the two diseases. Three possible judgements have been given below. Cross out two of them, leaving the one you think is most accurate and then say why you think that.

Overall I think there [was a lot of similarity / were many points of similarity / was only

a small amount of similarity] because ....

....

Activity

Below are extracts from two student answers. Choose the one relating to your extension study and:

- underline any spelling mistakes
- circle any errors of punctuation or grammar
- rewrite the extract with accurate spelling, punctuation and grammar on a separate sheet of paper.

Extension Study 1: Medicine and public health from Roman Britain to c.1350

the romans made many grate advansemants in public health coz they had extreamly strong goverment that had the power and organisation for large projects like aguaducts and baths, they could raise funds in taxs and had free manpower in slaves but in middle ages it was diffrent, they had small goverments that could not raise taxes or organise large public helth projecs. romans also wanted to keep there armys fit for war so public health was important for this, this was not the case in the middle ages. romans also learnt new skils and got knowlege from all over they're empire essecially the greeks but in the middle ages england were cut off and the knowlege were mostly lost, only sum remained in monasterys. but their were sum improvmants, in roman times hopsitals was just for woonded solders but in the middle ages munks and nuns ran hopsitals for evryone.

Extension Study 2: Public health c.1350 to present day

the goverments roll in improving public health was more impotant during the 19th centry than the 20th centry, this is becose in 1800s not many people new the risk of deseases and becose of this only the goverment could inforce cleanliness and improvments to public health. although the goverments roll was still impotant during 20th centry it was more impotant in the 19th centry becose this was when public health reform started and without the goverments input into things like public health acts this may never of happened eg the 1st public health act was in 1848 and in 1875 they made it compulsry, without these acts and others the improvment would of been delayed so what individuals did wouldn't of mattered without goverment to inforce it.

1B Crime and punishment

Unit 1 is a Development Study and therefore change and continuity are key themes in this paper. The 16-mark question comes in the Extension Studies, which cover two different periods:

- Extension Study 1 covers Crime and punishment from Roman Britain to c.1450
- Extension Study 2 covers Changing views of the nature of criminal activity using three case studies of witchcraft, conscientious objectors and domestic violence.

However, the examples used here will be based on material from the Core, Crime and Punishment c.1450 to present day. They will therefore be relevant to you whichever Extension Study you have covered, and you can make full use of them to practise your evaluation skills and essay planning.

Activity

1. Fill in the grid below showing the type of question and how to answer it for each of the questions. The first one has been done for you.

Question	Type	How to answer
Why was capital punishment abolished in 1969?	Orange	Explain how each of 3 or 4 points was a reason for its abolition
How similar were the Bow Street Runners and Peel's Metropolitan Police Force?		
Was car crime the biggest problem for the police in the twentieth century?		
How much did smuggling change in the period c.1700–c.2010?		
Who was more important in prison reform – John Howard or Elizabeth Fry?		
Why did the Tudors and Stuarts punish vagabonds so harshly?		
Did punishments change more in the nineteenth or twentieth century?		

Read the following question.

Who was more important in the reform of prisons – John Howard or Elizabeth Fry?

You may use the following in your answer and any other information of your own.

- 1777: John Howard published a report on the state of prisons in England and Wales.
- 1785: a new prison was built at Gloucester that incorporated many of Howard's recommendations.
- 1813: Fry visited the women's section of the prison at Newgate, London.

This is a 'scales' question. To answer this question properly you need to explain why Howard was important, why Fry was important, and then explain your judgement about who was more important.

Read Answer A below. It has all the necessary information but it is written as a narrative account and therefore would only be a Level 2 answer.

Answer A

John Howard became Sheriff of Bedfordshire in 1773 and when he inspected the prisons he found that they were dirty and crowded, the rich could pay to get private rooms and good food, female prisoners were often raped by the guards and young criminals mixed with older criminals, often learning new methods of crime. Howard carried out a detailed survey of all the prisons in England and Wales, measuring the space, checking the food and recording the fees system. He recommended that the gaolers should be paid to prevent them abusing the criminals, that prisoners should be separated according to their sex and according to their crimes, and that a doctor and a chaplain should visit regularly. He wanted prisoners to be reformed through education, religion and work so they could learn a trade and support themselves when they came out of prison, instead of going back to crime.

Elizabeth Fry was shocked to find that 300 women prisoners were crowded into three rooms at Newgate prison. She took in clean straw and clothes for the women and persuaded the prison authorities to set up a school for the children who were in prison. She also suggested changes such as female prison guards and the prisoners being taught a trade. She set up a chapel in the prison and introduced sewing as a compulsory activity for the women. Fry was invited to give evidence to parliament in 1818 but changes were not made until Peel's Gaol Act in 1823. She also toured prisons in England and Scotland and set up Ladies' Associations to visit prisoners and help improve conditions in other prisons.

To become a Level 3 answer these details need to be combined with an explanation showing why Howard and Fry were important in prison reform.

2. Match the comments and explanations in the table below to make explained comments.

1 .... 2 .... 3 .... 4 .... 5 ....

Comment about importance	Explanation
1. John Howard's position as High Sheriff was important because he ...	A. helped to improve conditions at other prisons.
2. Howard 's book publicised his findings which ...	B. parliament is the only organisation which can actually change the laws and enforce changes across the whole country.
3. Elizabeth Fry was important because she showed that ...	C. made people aware of the need for change and think about how to reform criminals.
4. Giving evidence to parliament was significant because ...	D. visited many prisons and realised that the problems and abuses were widespread.
5. Fry's Ladies' Associations ...	E. 30 years after Howard's report, conditions were still appalling in many prisons.

3. Now write your conclusion explaining who you think was more important. There is no 'right' answer here – excellent answers could explain why it was important that Howard was the first person to put pressure on the authorities to make changes, or why Fry's practical actions and support from others was important.

....

....

....

Activity

Read the following question and Answer B below.

How much change was there in the methods used to prevent crime and catch criminals in the period c.1500 – c.1900? (16 marks)

You may use the following in your answer and any other information of your own.

- In the sixteenth century towns and villages relied on unpaid constables and the 'hue and cry' to catch criminals.

- 1749: Bow Street Runners founded.

- 1878: Criminal Investigations Department set up.

Answer B

During the sixteenth century the 'hue and cry' was a system where anyone who witnessed a crime had to chase the criminal, shouting to draw attention to him so that other people would join in and help to catch the criminal. Each village had a constable, although he was not usually very efficient because he was appointed only for a year and was not paid. Towns often had nightwatchmen who were supposed to patrol the streets. They were not very effective even when new regulations about their duties were drawn up in the reign of Charles II. So the work of the Fielding brothers, who set up the Bow Street Runners and horse patrols in London during the eighteenth century, was a major change. For the first time there was a trained and paid group of men who were expected to track down and catch criminals. This idea was further developed by Robert Peel in 1829, when he set up the Metropolitan Police Force and in 1856 it became compulsory for every area of the country to have a professional police force. By 1900, the police had developed specialised groups such as the CID to solve crimes using new technology such as photographs and fingerprints. Therefore, there were huge changes in the ways criminals were caught during this period, developing from a system of unpaid and inefficient individuals to an organised professional, body.

There was also continuity because change only really began with the Fielding brothers' work in 1749. For most of this period, there was no real system of catching criminals or preventing crime. Furthermore, the Bow Street Runners and Peel's early police force only worked in the London area, so it was not until 1856 that changes happened that affected the whole country.

4. Below are three sets of marks and feedback. Highlight which mark and comment you think is the correct one for Answer B.

Top Level 2, 8 marks.
Lots of good detail about different aspects of law enforcement but little focus on change.

Top Level 3, 12 marks.
Good explanation of various examples of change and continuity in this period but no judgement about 'how much' change occurred.

Top Level 4, 16 marks.
Excellent examples of both change and continuity in methods used to catch criminals, and weighs up these two sides of the issue in order to reach a judgement.

Activity

Now have a look through the following question.

How similar were the social crimes of smuggling and poaching in the eighteenth century and the social crimes of smuggling and tax evasion in the twentieth century? (16 marks)

You may use the following in your answer and any other information of your own.

○ In the eighteenth century luxury items such as brandy, tea and silk were smuggled.

○ Poaching and smuggling in the eighteenth century were usually carried out at night.

○ When payments are made 'cash in hand' instead of being recorded through a bank, people can avoid paying tax on their earnings.

Remember that if you are being asked to compare and reach a judgement on 'how similar', you have to look at similarities and differences before you can weigh them up and decide.

5. Colour-code the points in the table, underlining similarities in blue and differences in red.

	Eighteenth century	Twentieth century
Nature of crime	Luxury goods smuggled to avoid paying tax as they come into the country; animals poached from someone's land to provide food.	Cigarettes and alcohol smuggled to avoid paying tax; illegal goods such as drugs or illegal immigrants also smuggled; earnings not declared to the tax office to avoid paying tax.
Methods	Carried out at night to avoid detection; smuggling and sometimes poaching done by organised gangs.	Not carried out at any specific time. Methods often involve technology, e.g. hidden compartments or computers.
Public attitudes towards the crime	Many respectable members of society bought smuggled goods; people often felt sympathy for poachers.	People usually hostile to organised smuggling or tax evasion but sometimes sympathetic to individual cases.

6. Now complete the following writing frame to write a good answer to this question.

There was a lot of similarity in the nature of the social crimes of the eighteenth and twentieth centuries. For example, ...

....

....

There were also similarities in the way these crimes were carried out. For example, ...

....

....

There were also similarities in the attitudes of other people towards these crimes ....

....

....

However, there were also some differences. For example, ...

....

....

Now see if you can improve your essay by writing a conclusion that weighs up both sides and reaches a judgement on how much similarity there was between the crimes in the two periods. Three possible judgements have been given. Cross out two of them, leaving the one you think is most accurate.

Overall I think there [was a lot of similarity / were many points of similarity / was only

a small amount of similarity] because ....

....

....

....

56

Activity

Below are extracts from two student answers. Choose the one relating to your extension study and:

- underline any spelling mistakes
- circle any errors of punctuation or grammar
- rewrite the extract with accurate spelling, punctuation and grammar on a separate sheet of paper.

Extension Study 1: Crime and punishment from Roman Britain to c.1450

law and order in england under the roman's and norman's was quiet similar cos many elements of the roman system remained the same during the norman rein such as wipping execution and fines as punishments as well as trials crimes and policing. the king or emperer in roman and norman times had abslute power and controlled everything and to be called a trator resulted in execution in both periods. there was no police forse in either periods but their were similar groups like vigils, urban cohortes and praitorian gard in roman times who did jobs like stopping riots and putting out fires and garding the emperer, and the norman's had hue and cry which meant that if you saw a crime comitted you had to announce it and the blood fued which meant that if someone killed your relative you had the right to kill them.

Extension Study 2: Changing views of the nature of criminal activity c.1450 to present day

concientous objecters were new criminels in wwl when conscription was brought in and those refusing to fight had to have a good reason to excuse them from fighting, pasifism was common with quakers and ecomonic and political reasons was also common but morel reasons was too. in wwl concientous objecters were treated as crimes if they wasn't excused from fighting, the public would give them white feathers simbolising that there cowards and the authorities sent them to prison. in 1916 many absolutists were sent to dartmor prison and some were sent to military prison's in france. some died in prison or afterwoods.

Here is an example of a change question from Unit 2.

> Why did the lives of cowboys change in the period 1865–80? (12 marks)
>
> You may use the following in your answer and any other information of your own.
>
> - 1866: about 260,000 cattle were driven from Texas to the rail-head at Sedalia.
> - In 1870 Charles Goodnight set up a ranch on the Great Plains.
> - In 1880 36,600 tonnes of barbed wire were made and sold.

This question is asking you to look at changes to the lives of cowboys in the years 1865–80. You need to think about what was happening to make changes to cowboys' lives during these years.

Activity

Look at Answer A below. It is a Level 2 answer (look at the mark scheme on page 44 to see why).

1. Underline where the answer DESCRIBES changes to the lives of cowboys in the years 1865–80.

2. Circle key specific and accurate information.

Answer A

The lives of cowboys changed a lot from 1865–1880. In 1865 after the end of the Civil War a lot of cattle ranchers came back to Texas and found that their cattle had grown to about 5 million. In 1866 the first cattle trail was set up and approximately 260,000 cattle were driven from Texas to the rail-head at Sedalia. There was not much demand for beef in Texas but there was a high demand in the northern states and therefore money could be made. Therefore ranchers set off on the long drive.

John Iliff realised that Texas Longhorns could survive the Plains' severe climate and so set up a ranch on the Great Plains. Then more ranchers set up on the Plains and cowboys began to move from Texas. In 1874 Glidden invented barbed wire. This ended the open range. In 1869 the first trans-continental railroad opened and this linked the east and west. Cowboys could now take their cattle to the railroads. This saved the cowboys a lot of time and effort and reduced their work.

Using words and phrases like 'because', 'so', 'therefore' and 'this meant that' are often very useful in helping you to write an answer that moves from DESCRIBING to EXPLAINING, improving the answer to a Level 3 answer.

3. Use these words and phrases to fill in the blanks for the statements below:

   a. Ranchers set off on the Long Drive .... there was more demand for beef in northern states .... money could be made.

   b. The opening of the first-transcontinental railroad was important as .... cowboys could now take their cattle to the railroads .... this saved them time and effort.

4. On a separate sheet of paper write an answer that EXPLAINS rather than DESCRIBES the different types of changes that happened to cowboys' lives in the years 1865–80.

Activity

Here is another question which focuses on change.

> What changes did the coming of railroads make to the development of the Great Plains? (12)
>
> You may use the following in your answer and any other information of your own.
>
> - 1869: The opening of the first trans-continental railroad.
>
> - Abilene was built on the Kansas – Pacific railroad.
>
> - Farming equipment was made in the eastern states.

Read Answer B below.

5. Underline the examples of specific and accurate information in this answer.

6. Cross out the parts of the answer that are irrelevant for this question.

Answer B

Before the coming of the railroads it was very difficult to cross the Great Plains. People had made very difficult and dangerous journeys by wagon train. The wagon trains could be made up of around 20 wagons. Sometimes this ended in disaster, like the Donner Party which had left in 1846. The wagon train got trapped in the severe weather and some of them only survived by being cannibals. By 1860 the US government were keen to help develop railroads for a number of reasons. As well as the idea of 'Manifest Destiny' the railroads would make it easier to solve problems of law and order as well as helping develop America's economy with the Far East. New cities grew on the western coast such as San Francisco. The railroads provided lots of jobs. New developments in machinery (such as wind pumps and barbed wire) which were made in the east could now be transported west. Homesteaders became much less isolated. Goods could be delivered to the west. The cattle industry also grew. The development of the railroads also had effects on the lives of the Plains Indians. It was much harder for the Plains Indians to hunt buffalo.

7. On a separate sheet of paper write an improved version of this answer by clearly explaining the changes brought to the Plains by the coming of the railroads.

Activity

Here is an example of the type of question 5(b) or 6(b) you will in get in the exam.

> 'Technology was the most important factor in solving the problems faced by homesteaders in the 1870s and 1880s.' Do you agree? Explain your answer. (16 marks)
>
> You may use the following in your answer and any other information of your own.

- 1869: The first railroad crossed the Great Plains.

- 1873: The US government passed the Timber and Culture Act.

- 1880s: Homesteaders started growing 'Turkey Red' wheat.

Hint

The first bullet point agrees with the statement in the question, whilst the other two bullet points give you another argument.

8. Read Answer C and then the four comments A–D below. Can you work out where each of the comments should go? Write the letter in the appropriate space.

Answer C

The homesteaders had many problems in the 1870s and 1880s. The land on the Plains was very dry in the summer, it had never been farmed before and the winters were severe. The Plains are a vast area and they lived very isolated lives. Many lived in sod houses – but it was very hard to keep these clean and hard to prevent the spreading of disease. There were also problems of plagues of locusts and grasshoppers. [......]

In 1862 the government passed the 1862 Homestead Act which allowed white settlers to claim some land – and they first started to become known as homesteaders. [......]

The homesteaders worked hard ploughing the land. It was hard work and they often had to dig wells. They used fences to show which land was theirs and to stop cattle destroying their crops. To begin with they mainly grew maize. They also faced problems such as plagues of grasshoppers in the 1870s.

Technology played a vital role in improving the homesteaders' lives. First of all the coming of the railroads meant that during the 1870s and 1880s their lives became less isolated. It also meant that manufactured goods and agricultural machinery (such as reapers and threshers) from the east could easily be transported and sold to the homesteaders. [......]

Technology also saw the invention of barbed wire in 1874 and this meant that homesteaders could farm their land without the danger of cattle damaging their land. This also meant that the homesteaders could farm more land easily without needing extra men. Other technology that helped homesteaders solve their farming problems was the availability of wind pumps by the 1880s. [......]

So technology played a major part in improving homesteaders' lives in the 1870s and 1880s. On the whole technology helped to solve a significant number of problems for the homesteaders.

A	Level 2: This is description of the lives of homesteaders.
B	Level 3: Here the student is explaining how technology helped the lives of homesteaders.
C	Here is another clear example of how technology helped the lives of homesteaders.
D	This is not relevant to this particular question – it is outside of the time frame.

Now read the evaluation question below.

> 'The Battle of Little Big Horn was a victory for the Plains Indians.' Do you agree? Explain your answer. (16 marks)
>
> You may use the following in your answer and any other information of your own.
>
> ● General Custer and more than 250 of his army officers were killed.
>
> ● Custer was seen as a hero by the American public.
>
> ● 1877: Crazy Horse was captured and later killed by the US army.

9. Read Answer D below and underline in red where you think it is Level 2 and in blue where you think it is Level 3.

Answer D

The Battle of Little Big Horn in 1876 was a major victory for the Plains Indians. There are many reasons why it can be seen as a major victory for the Plains Indians. First, the battle started when the whites found gold in the Black Hills and broke the Fort Laramie Treaty of 1868 which had stated that the whites would not go into what for the Indians was sacred land. This made the Indians very angry so they killed nearly 100 whites at Rosebud River. Then the army was sent in to protect the whites and kill the Indians but they foolishly split up their own army. When General Custer and his army of 250 located the Indians he charged in and his men were slaughtered. The Indians abandoned their traditions such as scalping and used quicker tactics, and many also had up-to-date Winchester rifles. This shows the mistakes made by Custer and showed the US army to be disorganised. Another reason why the Battle of Little Big Horn was a victory for the Plains Indians was that it united them. About 4,000 warriors gathered to fight Custer and his army.

The Indians defeated Custer in 1876 but in some ways this was not a final victory and the situation changed again in 1877.

10. Write another paragraph that looks at this 'other side' of the question to further improve Answer D.

....

....

....

....

....

....

....

Activity

Below is a student answer with a number of spelling, punctuation and grammar errors. Read the answer and then:

- underline any spelling mistakes
- circle any errors of punctuation or grammar
- rewrite the answer with accurate spelling, punctuation and grammar on a separate sheet of paper.

the coming of the railrode in 1865–85 was important to the growth of cattel ranshing, it meant more faster and easier access to heavily populated easten states, this is significant becose the beef could be sold where it is more in demand. also another reason of the growth of cattel ranshing was the cattel trails north. charles goodnight came back from the civil war to find his 180 cows had turned into 5000 longhorn's, charles goodnight and his assitant oliver loving decided to move the longhorn's north, this is important becose as the cattel trail north was successful other ranshs were influenced to do the same, the cattel ranshs made profit by going north. another reason was the cow towns, joseph mccoy was the 1st person to set up a cow town abilene, the development of the cow town meant cowboy's could have somewhere to stay while on cattel trails, the town also provided servises, socailising and cattel auctions. this is important becose it is creating more money for the cattel industry making it more powerful.

2C Life in Germany

Here is an example of a change question.

> In what ways did the lives of women in Nazi Germany change in the years 1933 to 1939? (12 marks)
>
> You may use the following in your answer and any other information of your own.
>
> - 1933: Law for the Encouragement of Marriage.
>
> - Education for girls stressed Domestic Science.
>
> - 1936: There was a shortage of workers in Germany.

This question is asking you to look at the changes to the lives of women in the years 1933 to 1939. You need to think about different types of changes that happen in women's lives during these years.

Activity

Look at Answer A below. It is a Level 2 answer (look at the mark scheme on page 44).

1. Underline where the answer DESCRIBES changes to women's lives.

2. Circle key specific and accurate information.

Answer A

The Nazis passed the Encouragement of Marriage Law in 1933. This gave a loan of 1,000 marks to every couple that got married and 200 marks for every child. The Nazi government also used propaganda to show what they believed women should do. The 3K's were 'cooking, children and church' and was what they wanted women to do. Posters were used to show that women were not supposed to wear short skirts or use make-up. The Nazis also introduced special medals for the number of children women had (bronze for four children, silver for six and gold for eight). Many women lost their jobs as teachers and working for the government. Girls were also taught their future roles as mothers in school with Domestic Science lessons which stressed their importance for the future of Germany. In 1936 more women were needed for work in factories.

Words and phrases like 'because', 'so', 'therefore' and 'this meant that' are often very useful in helping you to write an answer that improves the answer from DESCRIBING to EXPLAINING.

3. Use these words and phrases to fill in the blanks for the statements below.

> More women were encouraged to marry .... of the Encouragement of Marriage Law in 1933. For every child the family got 200 marks .... that they would have more children.
>
> Girls were taught Domestic Science in school .... the Nazi government wanted them to become good mothers. .... women were seen as very important for the future of Germany.

4. On a separate sheet of paper write an answer that EXPLAINS rather than DESCRIBES the changes to women's lives in Nazi Germany in the years 1933 to 1939.

Activity

Here is another question that focuses on change.

> In what ways did the Nazis' treatment of Jews change in the years 1938 to 1945? (12 marks)
>
> You may use the following in your answer and any other information of your own.
>
> - November 1938: German Jews and property were attacked during Kristallnacht (Night of the Broken Glass).
>
> - 1939: The beginning of the Second World War.
>
> - 1942: The use of Zyklon B gas at Auschwitz.

Now read Answer B below.

5. Underline the examples of specific and accurate information in this answer.

6. Cross out the parts of the answer that are irrelevant for this question.

Answer B

Soon after Hitler became Chancellor of Germany the Nazis ordered the one-day boycott of Jewish shops. They had signs outside saying that anybody using these shops were traitors to Germany. Following this the Nuremberg Laws were passed and this made sexual relations and marriage between 'pure' Germans and Jews illegal. After the murder of Von Rath, Kristallnacht occurred and many German Jews were attacked and their properties, businesses and places of worship were destroyed. The Jews were even ordered to pay compensation for the attacks on their property. A year later the Second World War broke out. The Nazis used their special Einsatzgruppen forces who killed many Jews in Eastern Europe. Also many Jews were forced to live in ghettos such as the one in Warsaw. Here many died of disease (such as typhus) and lack of food. In January 1942 Nazis met at Wannsee where the planning of the 'Final Solution' was discussed and it was decided to build death camps. Over the next two years train loads of Jews from many European countries were sent to these camps. On arrival at the camps, SS officers divided the prisoners into those for immediate death and the others were used for slave labour. By the end of the Second World War, 6 million European Jews had been killed by the Nazis.

7. On a separate sheet of paper now write an improved version of this answer by clearly explaining the changes to the Nazis' treatment of Jews from 1938 to 1945.

Activity

Here is an example of the type of question 5(b) or 6(b) you will in get in the exam.

> 'The main role of education in Nazi Germany was to prepare boys and girls for different roles.' Do you agree? Explain your answer. (16 marks)
>
> You may use the following in your answer and any other information of your own.
>
> - Girls studied Domestic Science. ○ Boxing was compulsory in school for boys.
>
> - All pupils had lessons in Race Studies.

8. Read Answer C and then the four comments A–D below. Can you work out where each of the comments should go? Write the letter in the appropriate space.

Hint

Notice that the first two bullet points agree with the statement in the question. The final point gives you another argument.

Answer C

I agree with the statement that the main role of education in Nazi Germany was to prepare boys and girls for different roles. There were different timetables for boys and girls. For example, boys were taught more PE and girls had more lessons in subjects such as Domestic Science. This was because the Nazis wanted the girls to grow up and be fit and healthy and so have healthy children. [......]

The boys were being prepared for their future roles in the armed forces. There were even special Adolf Hitler Schools which were to prepare future Nazi leaders. So the Nazis were using education to prepare boys and girls for their future roles. This happened outside of schools too and in the Hitler Youth and the League of German Maidens. In the youth groups boys again were taught more skills to prepare them as future soldiers and the girls as future mothers. [......]

Later on there would be marriage loans so that more women would give up their work and also they would get medals for the number of children they had.

However, both boys and girls were taught Race Studies. This was so that the Nazis could spread what they believed about the Jews. This included learning things such as what Jews looked like and blaming them for Germany's problems. [......]

As well as Race Studies, both boys and girls would learn Nazi ideas in other subjects such as Maths, German and History. In these lessons they would learn about how many bombs were needed for bombing other countries, Germany's need for expansion into the East and the unfairness of the Treaty of Versailles. [......]

Therefore, in conclusion, I agree with the statement that education was mainly to prepare boys and girls for different roles, but it was also used to spread their ideas about race.

A	Level 2: This is description of Nazi education policies.
B	Level 3: Here the student is explaining Nazi education policies.
C	Level 3: Here is another clear example of an explanation of Nazi education policies.
D	This is not relevant to this particular question – this is not related to education, but youth.

Activity

Now read the evaluation question below.

'The Wall Street Crash was the most important reason for the increase in support for the Nazis in the years 1928–1932.' Do you agree? Explain your answer. (16 marks)

You may use the following in your answer and any other information of your own.

- 1928: The Nazis had less than 3 per cent of the vote.
- 1932: A Nazi election poster had the caption 'Hitler – Our Last Hope!'
- 1932: Unemployment in Germany reached 6 million.

9. Read Answer D below and underline in red where you think it is Level 2 and in blue where you think it is Level 3.

Answer D

Yes I agree that the Wall Street Crash was the most important reason for the increase in support for the Nazis in the years 1928 to 1932. This is because until the Wall Street Crash, the Weimar Republic was on the road to recovery. The Wall Street Crash was when the Stock Exchange suddenly collapsed in New York. This meant that the USA could no longer lend Germany money but also ordered all the loans to Germany to be paid back immediately. This meant that businesses went bankrupt and so unemployment started rising in Germany. Many Germans began turning to the Nazi Party. By 1932 unemployment reached 6 million. Many Germans were living in desperate poverty and were even using soup kitchens in major cities such as Berlin. This is when the Nazis gained much more support. Nazi propaganda posters were used such as 'Hitler! Our last hope.' Many of the working class believed that Hitler would improve things and provide jobs. Therefore the Wall Street Crash created a lot of problems in the German economy and Hitler could take advantage of this. The Nazis were able to use clever techniques to get many different people voting for them and by 1932 the Nazis were the largest political party in the Reichstag.

They system of proportional representation used in elections in Germany meant that the government was a mixture of different political parties, so they found it hard to agree on policies.

10. Write an extra paragraph that looks at this 'other side' of the question to further improve Answer D.

....

....

....

....

....

....

Activity

Below is a student answer with a number of spelling, punctuation and grammar errors. Read the answer and:

- underline any spelling mistakes
- circle any errors of punctuation or grammar
- rewrite the answer with accurate spelling, punctuation and grammar on a separate sheet of paper.

the wall st crash was the most important reason for the incraese in support for the nazi's in 1928–32 as germany was too reliant on america and the nazi's need kaos to help them get more votes. in 1932 umenployment rose to 6m people becose of the wall st crash as employer's didn't have that much money to give out, the nazi's also used propoganda like radio broadcasts newspapers and posters to publish the fact that germany is becoming kaotic and hilter has the answer. before the wall st crash happened the nazi's only had less than 3% of votes which wasn't alot becose germany wasn't in an awful state, it still had a chance to be great again. after the crash umenployment had rose to 6m german people and hilter and the nazi's could use this to there advantage and they promised that when the nazi's are in power people will have jobs again, as a result of the promises they made the nazi's got more votes. the nazi's could also advetise that hilter was they're best hope through propoganda, cleverly using the kaos from the wall st crash. when hilter did his speech's he only spoke about what people wanted to hear like an end to inflation and end to umenployment. the nazi's needed something really bad like the wall st crash to happen to be able to get into power.

Unit 3 Introduction

What is Unit 3 about?

Unit 3 is a source enquiry unit. There are four options in this unit and you will be studying one of them. This book covers the following two options. Highlight the option you have studied:

- Option 3A: The transformation of surgery c.1845–c.1918

- Option 3B: Protest, law and order in the twentieth century

What do I need to know?

You have to answer five questions, each testing different source skills, including:

- making supported inferences (see pages 76–81)

- explaining the message or purpose of a source (see pages 76–81)

- cross-referencing three sources (see pages 82–86)

- evaluating the utility of two sources (see pages 87–93)

- using sources and own knowledge to reach a judgement (see pages 94–100).

The knowledge that you have about the topic is called contextual knowledge and you must make use of it in question 5. However, it will also help you with your source skills because:

- it will ensure that you understand what the source is suggesting

- it will enable you to make judgements about the source itself – how accurate it is; how well it has covered the event.

What will the exam paper be like?

You have 75 minutes to answer this exam paper. It is worth 53 marks. You will be given a Source Booklet with six to eight sources (labelled A–H) on a topic within your option. They will be a mixture of written sources and illustrations. You have to answer five questions on these sources.

- Question 1 is an inference question on Source A and is worth 6 marks.

- Question 2 is a source analysis question on Source B; it is focused on portrayal and is worth 8 marks.

- Question 3 is a cross-referencing/comparison question and is worth 10 marks; it will usually involve at least one source you have already used and at least one new one, for example, Sources B, C and D.

- Question 4 will ask you to compare the utility or value of two sources and is worth 10 marks.

- Question 5 will give you an issue or comment ('hypothesis') and ask you to use three sources and your contextual knowledge to reach a judgement. It is worth 16 marks. There are also up to 3 additional marks available in this question for spelling, punctuation and grammar.

The guidance on the next two pages gives you an overview of the key source skills you'll need to use in the source paper. You will then look at each question type in turn to help you to practise those skills on sources which are suitable for the option you are studying.

Source skills

You will need to make use of a variety of skills when you answer source questions. These include annotating sources, making use of the contents of sources and of your contextual knowledge and understanding, as well as being able to apply the criteria of nature, origins and purpose of sources. These are shown in the following examples.

Annotating sources

First of all read the question before you look at the relevant source or sources. This will ensure that you make full use of the source. You may find it useful to annotate the sources as you read them, either by highlighting or underlining the information. Remember to also make use of the information given above the source which is known as the provenance. For example, who produced the source and when and what type of source it is. In a written source, you should highlight the key words or phrases in the source itself. In illustrations, you should highlight the key features and people shown.

This will help you to work out what the source is suggesting.

Contextual knowledge

This means the knowledge that you have about a topic or event. This knowledge will help you with your source skills because:

- it will ensure that you understand what the source is suggesting

- it will enable you to make judgements about the source itself – how accurate it is, how well it has covered the event.

For example, using Source A overleaf, it would be helpful to know that the poster was produced during the Second World War at a time when Britain was alone in facing Germany and Italy. Winston Churchill was popular with most British people because of his determination not to surrender.

Contents

This is the information which the source gives you about an event or person. You will need to identify information such as dates and actual events as well as opinions and points of view. For example, in Source A you can see:

- Winston Churchill, the Prime Minister, in the foreground

- a catchy slogan

- tanks and fighter planes in the background.

The nature, origins and purpose of sources

This approach helps you to make use of the provenance of the source and why the source was produced.

Source A: A poster issued by the British government in late 1940

Nature

This means the type of source. Is it a poster, photograph, cartoon, speech, diary, letter?

This is a poster. Posters are usually produced for propaganda purposes to persuade people to think or act in a certain way.

Origins

This means when was the source produced and by whom.

This was produced by the British government in late 1940.

Purpose

This means why was the source produced. What is it trying to make you do? Who is it trying to make you support?

This is an example of a propaganda poster which is trying to get support for the Prime Minister and the war effort and to keep up the morale of the British people.

Source A: The Old Operating Theatre at St Thomas's Hospital, London. This room was bricked up in the mid-nineteenth century but rediscovered in 1956 and restored to show how it would have appeared.

Source B: From an account by the Professor of Chemistry at Edinburgh University, describing Simpson's attempts to find a better anaesthetic than ether.

> On one occasion he came into my laboratory to ask whether I had any new substance likely to produce anaesthesia. My assistant had just prepared a liquid which I thought worthy of experiment. Simpson, who was brave to the point of rashness in his experiments, wished to try it upon himself. This I absolutely refused to allow, and declined to give him any of the liquid unless he promised me first to try its effect on rabbits. Two rabbits were brought, and under the vapour quickly passed into anaesthesia, coming out of it in due course. Next day, Simpson proposed to experiment upon himself and his assistant with this liquid but the assistant suggested that they should first see how the rabbits had fared. They were both found to be dead.

Source C: From a letter by Dr Liston, after he had used ether on patients during two operations.

> I tried the ether inhalation today in a case of amputation of the thigh, and in another on the great toe-nail, which is one of the most painful operations in surgery. In both operations I had the most perfect and satisfactory results. It is a very great thing to be able to destroy pain to such an extent, and without, apparently, any bad result. It is a fine thing for operating surgeons.

Source D: From a report of a speech by Professor Syme, a leading surgeon, to the Medical Society of Edinburgh in 1849. He is speaking here about the use of chloroform in surgery.

After it was proposed by Dr. Simpson, Syme used it in the first operation he had to perform in the hospital and ever since then he had continued to use it. He desired to state to the Society that he believed anaesthesia not only saved patients operated on from pain, but also from shock, and all its effects. When Dr. Simpson first stated this as his opinion, Mr Syme had strongly opposed it but now he was convinced that Dr Simpson was right.

Source E: From a report in *The Lancet*, a medical journal, published on 22 December 1849.

An inquest* was held at Shrewsbury upon the body of a poor Welsh girl. It appeared that it was necessary for her to undergo a very painful operation, the removal of the eyeball. The surgeon administered about one-third of the quantity of chloroform he has given to other patients. It had, however, such an effect upon her that she was seized with apoplexy**. The jury returned a verdict of 'Died by apoplexy, caused by inhaling chloroform'.

    * An inquest is an investigation into why someone died

    ** Apoplexy was often used to describe a stroke

Source F: An illustration showing the unveiling of a statue of Simpson in Edinburgh, 1877.

Source A: A leaflet describing the force-feeding of suffragettes in a Liverpool prison in December, 1909.

At night she was kept in irons. Next day she was thrown down with her face upon the floor. Face downwards, her arms and legs were dragged up until she was lifted from the ground. Her hair was seized by another wardress. In this way she was marched up the steps her head bumping on the stone stairs. In the room the operation of forcible feeding was performed - causing a terrible state of physical and mental distress. She was handcuffed again, flung down the steps and pushed and dragged back into her cell.

The frog march, and the other assaults and cruelties, the brutal feeding by force, were resorted to while she was an unconvicted prisoner. Prison officials, encouraged by the Government, have cast aside both law and humanity in dealing with women political prisoners.

Source B: A letter written to a newspaper "The Dundee Advertiser," in 1913.

To the Editor of the Dundee Advertiser.

Sir, I would suggest to the authorities that the next time the suffragettes decide to riot and disturb a public meeting the water hose should be turned upon them. A few firemen could be put behind the barricades, then when the "high-bred" hooligans, followed by a horde of low-bred hooligans, came surging along the firemen can simply cool their feverish frenzy and break no bones. The women would quickly melt away like the mist of the morning. No need for a hunger strike or mounted police. The cold water would cure them completely, and save taxpayers a lot of expense.,

A.D., HOOLIGAN HATER

Source C: An account of the 1984 Miners' Strike on a website.

Bitter disputes remain over the tactics used; the use of the Metropolitan Police in local mining villages, accusations of biased newspapers, flying pickets to discourage strike breakers from working. As the demonstrating grew there were violent confrontations between pickets and police. A key confrontation was the 'Battle of Orgreave' when one mass picket on 18th June 1984 was 10,000 strong and the pickets were met with police in riot gear, police horses and dogs. The strike also saw mass meetings and great marches where dockers and railway workers joined miners. However, opinion was divided about the violence and tragedies which occurred, for example the death of one flying picket and when a taxi driver died taking two 'scab' miners to work in South Wales after a concrete post was dropped from a bridge onto his car.

Source D: An extract from a 2010 article by David Whetstone on Journallive.co.uk reviewing the book *No Redemption* which looks at the difficulties faced by the families of miners during the strike.

History records that they did, indeed, get past Christmas. The union's area executive ensured that every family got a turkey and a tenner, but others rallied round to ensure miners' children didn't get overlooked by Santa.

The close-knit nature of the old mining communities ensured that nobody starved or froze. Marilyn remembered how she and other wives kept the kitchen going and also advised women in other mining areas how to get one started. She recalled many acts of support and generosity, from the old man who came in to put a fiver in the strike fund to the Durham University students who donated food

Source E: A painting by John Bartlett of the Poll Tax riots in Trafalgar Square on 31 March 1990. The painting is now displayed in the Museum of London.

Source F: An account of the Poll Tax Riots by a demonstrator who was arrested.

Eyewitness account of Anti-poll Tax Riot

I arrived in Trafalgar Square to see riot police attacking demonstrators with batons and shields. But people were not taking it. They fought back with whatever they could find. One police officer got separated from his group. He was cornered by the theatre on Whitehall. Someone lifted the visor on his crash helmet and punched him in the face. He dropped. Then the police horses charged, supported by police vans. But the crowd was so big they could not force their way through.

Not long after that one of the buildings in Trafalgar Square was set on fire. The heat from the fire became so intense it was dangerous to stay in the square. I marched with about 2000 other demonstrators to Piccadilly Circus and then up Regent's Street. We wanted to get to the BBC to demand they broadcast the truth about the protest.

As we walked up Regent's Street all you could hear was the sound of breaking glass. Looters, young and old, smashed the huge plate glass windows of all the posh designer shops. Ordinary shoppers who hadn't even been on the demonstration joined in. It was a like a scene from a revolution. There was a jubilant atmosphere. We hated Thatcher and now the whole world knew it!

Inference and portrayal questions

Unit 3 tests your evidence skills by giving you an enquiry to carry out, based on a set of sources. You are expected to know somthing about the topic and that will help you to understand the sources, but you do not need to use your own knowledge in your answers until question 5.

Question 1: Inference

In Unit 3, question 1 will always ask you 'What can you learn from Source A about …?' It is an inference question and you answer it in the same way as the inference question in Unit 2.

- You need to work out something that is not stated in the source, for example, people's attitude, the fact that something was difficult or an overall impression.

- You also need to show which bit of the source you have used to make that inference.

The only difference is that in Unit 3 the inference question is worth 6 marks and therefore you need to make and support **TWO** inferences.

The question is about making inferences from the source, so remember that you shouldn't use your own knowledge. You should also not waste time describing the source . The examination answer booklet will give you two sides of paper for this question, but you should not need more than one side to make and support two inferences from the source.

Question 2: Portrayal

In Unit 3, question 2 is about portrayal – the way something is presented and the impression it creates. The source can be a visual or a written source. The question can be worded in various ways.

- How does the artist convey his message?

- What impression is created in Source B?

- Why do you think this painting was done?

- How can you tell the author of Source B disapproves of the situation?

In your answer, you need to analyse different parts of the source, showing how individual details have been used to create a particular impression.

In other words...

When you see a trailer for a new film, the clips that you see have all been selected to create the impression that the film is funny, scary, or exciting in order to make you want to see the film. If you read a review for the film, the points the reviewer makes and the words the reviewer has chosen all build up to create a positive or negative impression, to help you decide whether to see the film.

Analysing portrayal is all about identifying these individual elements and showing how they work together to create an overall impression.

How will I be marked?

Portrayal questions are worth 8 marks and the mark scheme has three levels.

Level	Mark	Answer
1	1–2	The answer makes a valid comment about the message or portrayal in the source OR the answer writes about details from the source but does not link these to the message or impression created.
2	3–5	The answer makes a valid comment about the message or impression created and links this to details from the source.
3	6–8	The answer analyses the way the source details build up to create a message or impression, either through the choice of details to include and leave out, or the treatment and way the detail is presented.

Good answers for question 2 focus on the choice of details to include and the way they are used to create a particular impression.

- In a visual source, for example, you might comment on the way items or people are grouped in the picture, the way light and colour are used to draw your attention, the expressions on people's faces, and so on.

- In a written source, you should comment on the language used and the way that the author has organised their points. For example, does the author emphasise all the positive points and cover negative ones only very briefly at the end?

Remember

Avoid lengthy descriptions of the source: there is no point in simply repeating the information.

- You don't need to evaluate the source for reliability – the mark scheme for portrayal has no marks for this as it's covered in a separate question.

- Don't write about the situation from your own knowledge in this question – you're being asked about the impression created in this source.

In Unit 3A the sources are all about developments in surgery during a key period (c.1845–c.1918). At the start of this period, operations were painful and often fatal, so people agreed to have surgery only when they were desperate. Because operations were so painful, they had to be carried out as quickly as possible and this meant that only basic operations could be carried out. The first question sometimes asks about the problems of surgery as a way of 'setting the scene' before you go on to look at changes.

Question 1: Inference

Here's an example of an exam-style question asking you to look at a source.

> What can you learn from Source A about the way operations were carried out in the mid-nineteenth century? (6 marks)

Activity

1. Use Source A (on page 71) to add supporting evidence for the three inferences below. Remember that your own knowledge will help you to understand the details you can see in Source A but your answer has to be based on the source.

There were spectators at many operations. I can work this out from the fact that ......

....

....

The conditions were unhygienic. This is shown by ....

....

....

The equipment was basic. This inference is supported by ....

....

....

Read Answer A below.

Answer A

In Source A there is a wooden table where the patient was held down while the operation was done. The surgeon's coat is hanging on the wall. There are also places for spectators to stand and watch. I can tell from Source A that operations were painful. They were so painful that operations had to be done as quickly as possible and the danger from infection and bloodloss meant that people did not agree to have an operation unless they were desperate.

2. Remind yourself of the mark scheme on page 77 and use it to decide which one of the comments below you think is the right one for this answer. Circle your choice.

Level 3	The answer makes an inference about problems in surgery and uses specific details from the source to support that inference.
Level 2	The answer makes a valid comment about surgery in the mid-nineteenth century and links it to a comment about the source.
Level 1	The answer describes some details in the source but the comments about surgery are all from own knowledge and cannot be linked to the source.

Activity

Question 2: Portrayal

Here is an example of a 'portrayal' question.

What impression of the anaesthetic is given in Source B? (8 marks)

Read Answer B below, which would be a Level 3 answer.

3. Underline the places where the answer shows how the choice of words creates an impression of the anaesthetic.

4. Circle the places where the answer shows how the treatment of the detail creates an impression of the anaesthetic.

Answer B

Source B creates the impression that the anaesthetic is a new discovery and it is dangerous. The author says the assistant 'had just prepared a liquid which I thought worthy of experiment'. Saying 'just prepared' suggests that it was a brand new mixture and 'worthy of experiment' shows they hadn't tested it before. The idea that it was dangerous is shown by the way that the author insisted on trying it out on rabbits before letting Simpson test it and by the dramatic way he says that the rabbits had died.

5. Read Source B on page 71 carefully and then finish the sentences below to build an answer to the following question.

What impression of Simpson is given in Source B? (8 marks)

The source shows Simpson is daring and adventurous by the use of words such as ....

....

This impression is backed up by the way it mentions ....

....

....

3B Protest, law and order

In Unit 3B the sources deal with one or more of these four key protests in Britain during the twentieth century: the suffragettes, the General Strike, the Miners' Strike and the poll tax protests.

You will have looked at the causes, the leadership, the methods used by protestors and the results for each of these four case studies. You will also have learnt about how the authorities responded to these protests and the role of the economy, politics and the media in each of them. Some of the main issues you should think about are:

- if the methods and tactics used by protestors helped to achieve or hindered their aims
- the various methods used by the authorities in dealing with protest
- the role of the media in influencing peoples' opinions about protest
- the impact that the economy and political issues may have had on the protest.

Activity

Question 1: Inference

Now let's look at an example of an inference question.

> What can you learn from Source A about how the authorities treated the suffragettes?
> (6 marks)

Remember

Your own knowledge will help you to understand the details you can see in Source A but your answer has to be based on the source.

1. Use Source A on page 73 to provide supporting evidence for the three inferences below.

The suffragettes were treated very harshly by the authorities. I can work this out from the fact that ....

....

....

....

The authorities were against the suffragettes. This is shown by ....

....

....

....

The suffragettes were treated badly by the authorities. This inference is supported by

....

....

....

2. Use the mark scheme on page 77 to decide what Level you think Answer A is, explaining your reasons.

Answer A

In Source A the suffragette was pulled by her hair. Other women were handcuffed and another was held in irons. The women were also force fed and they were treated this way before they had been to court. The way they were treated by the prison staff was harsh.

I think this answer is a Level .... answer because ....

....

....

3. Now underline where the answer has made a valid inference.

4. Finally, improve the answer by supporting the inference made directly from the source.

I can tell that the suffragettes were treated harshly by the authorities because ....

....

....

Activity

Question 2 : Portrayal

Here is an example of a portrayal-style question.

> How can you tell that the author of Source B disapproves of the suffragettes? (8 marks)

Read Answer B below, which would be a Level 3 answer, and complete the following tasks.

5. Underline the places where the answer shows how the choice of words creates an impression that the author disapproves of the suffragettes.

6. Circle the places where the answer shows how the treatment of the detail creates an impression of disapproval of the suffragettes.

Answer B

The author of Source B disapproves of the suffragettes. The source says that they 'riot and disturb' in quite large numbers and he uses the word 'horde'. This gives the impression that he thinks they are acting in an uncivilised manner and that they create problems. The author uses 'high-bred' in a sarcastic way to give the impression that the suffragettes think that they are high-class and well-bred but the author thinks that they are acting in a disrespectful way. He also shows how he thinks money should be saved and taxpayers should be saved 'a lot of expense.'

Cross-referencing questions

Question three in Unit 3 will usually tell you to use three sources and decide how far a given comment is supported by the evidence of those sources. This is known as cross-referencing between sources. It might be a comment from one of the sources or an overall statement, but there will be points where the sources agree and points where they disagree.

Hint

In any question that asks 'how far', you always need to consider both sides of the issue before you make your judgement.

How do I answer cross-referencing questions?

Read all the sources for this question carefully before you start writing your answer, even if you've used one or more of the sources in an earlier question.

When you are cross-referencing between sources, you need to look at the following.

- How far the details of each source support or challenge the idea being tested.
- How far the sources have a similar attitude/tone towards the idea being tested.
- How much weight to put on individual sources.

In other words...

You hear a rumour that school will finish early today, so you check it by asking three people. Two students say school will close early – one says it will close at 1pm and the other says at 2.30pm – but a teacher says it won't. The fact that the two students don't agree on the details makes it unlikely that school is closing early but you also put extra weight on the teacher's view because you would expect them to be in a position to know the truth.

How will I be marked?

This question will always be worth 10 marks which are spread across three levels. The below shows Level 2 and Level 3.

Level	Marks	Descriptor
2	3–6	Answer matches the detail of the sources to find examples of support or challenge OR answer evaluates sources for reliability.
3	7–10	Answer carefully analyses and weighs up the extent and importance of support and challenge between the sources OR answer evaluates sources for reliability in order to consider the weight of each source as evidence.

Remember that it will take you a bit of time to go through all the details of each source and to think about how much weight to place on the evidence. If you write a brief plan at this stage, you should only need another ten minutes to write a detailed answer that makes a judgment based on the evidence of the sources.

There is no 'right' answer for these questions but you cannot write a Level 3 answer by just matching details; you have to consider the overall weight of the evidence on each side of the issue.

Cross-referencing questions

Let's start with an example using just two sources.

> How far do Sources B and C suggest that Simpson deserves the credit for solving the problem of pain in surgery? (10 marks)

Activity

Read Answer A below. This is a Level 1 answer. All it does is describe each source.

Answer A

Source B tells us how Simpson was willing to experiment on himself in an attempt to find an anaesthetic. He was so keen that he was prepared to try dangerous new mixtures even before they had been tested on animals. However, Source C tells us that Dr Robert Liston had used ether and found that it was an effective anaesthetic. He talks about it giving 'perfect and satisfactory results' and about how pleased he is that he has destroyed pain.

1. Now read the two possible additions to Answer A below. For each one, explain why it would improve the answer.

Source B is very reliable. It comes from the Professor of Chemistry at Edinburgh University. He is talking about something he saw himself and the source suggests that he knew Simpson quite well and that Simpson did these experiments quite often. He has no reason to lie or exaggerate.

This would make the answer a Level 2 answer because ....

....

....

Source B says Simpson was experimenting to find an anaesthetic which supports the idea that he deserves the credit for solving the problem of pain. The Professor of Chemistry at Edinburgh is writing from his own knowledge and would have no reason to lie about this, so Source B is quite strong evidence. However, Source C says Liston used ether. Source C seems accurate and reliable because Liston is so pleased about the way ether works and has no reason to lie but it contradicts B and suggests that Simpson was not completely responsible for solving the problem of pain.

This would make the answer a Level 3 answer because ....

....

....

It is always worth spending time planning the answer to the cross-referencing question.

2. Fill in the table below using Sources B and D.

	Source B	Source D
Source content about Simpson and the discovery of anaesthetics	Simpson was experimenting to find an anaesthetic Simpson wanted to test mixtures on himself before he knew they were safe	
Points of similarity		Simpson is shown as being very keen to use anaesthetics and passing on his ideas
Points of difference	B does not say that Simpson was successful	
Points about reliability		Speaking from personal experience No reason to lie

3. Now put all this work together and, on a separate sheet of paper, write an answer to the following question.

How far do Sources B, C and D suggest that Simpson deserves the credit for solving the problem of pain in surgery? (10 marks)

Cross-referencing questions

Let's start with an example using two sources on the Poll Tax riots.

> How far do Sources E and F suggest that the police used violence during the protests? Explain your answer, using these sources. (10 marks)

Activity

Read Answer A below. This is a Level 1 answer – all it does is describe each source.

Answer A

Source F tells us that the police used horses. Source F also says that the police used 'weapons'. In Source E you can see the police attacking the protestors and they are in riot gear. So the sources all say that the police used violence.

Now read the Answers B and C below.

Answer B

Source F says the police used 'batons and shields' and also says that the 'police horses charged'. This tells us that the police clearly did use violence. The picture in Source E also shows the police using batons, riot gear and horses.

1. Look back at the mark scheme on page 82. Explain why Answer B is a Level 2 answer.

....

....

....

....

Answer C

Source F says the police used 'batons and shields' and also says that the 'police horses charged'. However Source F is from a protestor, who could be exaggerating the violence by the police because he is against the Poll Tax. The picture in Source E also shows the police using batons, riot gear and horses but it is not clear whether the police are actually defending themselves.

2. Look back at the mark scheme on page 82. Explain why Answer C is a Level 3 answer.

....

....

....

....

It is always worth spending time planning the answer to the cross-referencing question.

3. Fill in the table below using Sources E and F to plan an answer comparing these two sources.

	Source E	Source F
Source content about the police and the use of violence		A description of the fighting between the police and protestors and details of what happened elsewhere.
Points of similarity	There is a police van, a fire bomb going off and the police are using batons, shields and horses.	
Points of difference	This is only about what happened in Trafalgar Square and you can't tell who is the most to blame for the violence.	
Points about reliability		
How much weight can be placed on this evidence?		An eyewitness account from personal knowlege.

4. Now put all this work together and, on a separate piece of paper, write an answer to the following question.

How far do Sources E and F suggest that the police used violence during these protests? Explain your answer, using these sources. (10 marks)

Source evaluation questions

Question 4 in Unit 3 asks you to look at two sources and decide which is the more useful or valuable to the historian.

A source's usefulness or value depends partly on how much of the source content is relevant for the historian's enquiry. For example, a source may provide new detail about an event but not explain someone's motives for their actions or show people's attitudes. Another source might have less detail about what happened but give the historian a better understanding of how people felt.

Equally important is the reliability of the source – can you trust the information? Ask yourself these questions.

- Does the person who produced this source **know** the full truth?

- Is the person who created this source **telling** the full truth?

In other words...

If there was a fight at school, the teachers would try to find out how it started. It is likely that each of the people involved would blame the other one but it also likely that their friends would take sides as well. The teachers would therefore try to find someone who is not a friend of either of the people involved to get a more reliable account of what happened.

How do I answer source evaluation questions?

Check the question carefully – what are you being asked to use the source for? Is the historian investigating why an event happened, how important it was or the attitudes of the public? Look at the content and see how the historian could use the information for that purpose.

Then consider factors affecting reliability. This is often done by looking at the nature, origins and purpose of the source.

- **Nature** – What sort of source is it and how does that affect its reliability? For example, diaries reflect the writer's personal feelings but are not necessarily accurate records of events; some newspapers sensationalise in order to interest their readers although the basic facts should be accurate.

- **Origins** – Does the source come from someone involved who should know what they are talking about?

- **Purpose** – Was the source written to persuade people? Did the author set out to criticise someone or justify his own actions, has the historian tried to find out the full truth about an event?

Remember

Reliability does not depend on how many details there are in the source (they could be made up), or whether it is a primary source. Even eyewitness accounts are not automatically reliable as people may not know the full details.

The source might also be accurate and reliable but simply one example which was not typical of the situation. When you're considering the reliability of a source you should do the following.

- Look carefully at the language of the source – does the author claim to know all the details? Do any of the words suggest the author has strong feelings on the issue?

- Use any information you have been given in the caption – for example, if the author was involved; if they wrote it at a much later date; if they were paid to produce the source.

- Then consider whether the source information matches with what you already know.

A good answer can actually be quite short if it is well focused, so it is worth making brief notes before you begin your answer. For example:

	Source A	Source B
Usefulness of source content		
Reliability		

How will I be marked?

This question is worth 10 marks and you should spend about 15 minutes on it.

Level	Marks	Descriptor
1	1–3	Answer decides the value of the source on a simple basis, e.g. A tells you more than B; B is from an historian who wasn't there at the time.
2	4–7	Answer decides the value of the source by showing which source's information helps the historian more OR by showing which source is more reliable.
3	8-10	Answer shows how the reliability of a source affects the value of the information it contains.

The best answers to question 4 say very clearly what use the historian will make of the information in the source and whether it has any added weight because of its origins or reliability. For example:

- Source A tells me a lot about why he was doing this and since it is coming from the person themselves I assume we can trust the information, which makes this source very useful for explaining their actions

- Source B, which is a newspaper report describing events, gives me a good sense of why this was important. I realise that newspapers sometimes sensationalise their articles but the language here doesn't sound very extreme so I think this information can be trusted.

The most important thing is to use the details of the source in your answer. Don't talk about newspapers exaggerating or a source being biased unless you can back it up with an example from the source.

Remember

There is no 'right' answer to these questions but you need to show how the reliability of a source affects how much weight the historian can put on the information it contains. The following table shows the ways in which the nature or origin of a source can strengthen or weaken its value to the historian.

Source type	How reliability strengthens the value of the source content	How reliability weakens the value of the source content
Personal source (diary, letter)	The source will not be checked, so there is no reason to lie and it can offer extra information or explanation from someone involved.	The source will be from one person's perspective and could exaggerate their own importance or give a slanted view of other people.
Public source (newspaper, poster, cartoon)	It will contain the key points and because it is intended to appeal to people it probably reflects public attitudes.	Facts will be presented in a certain way, e.g. using loaded language, which could create a misleading impression.
Official sources (government records)	They are likely to be based on accurate facts and they show the views of the government.	The details may have been selected or presented in a certain way in order to get public support.
Media sources (photograph, newsreels or films from the time, etc.)	A photograph or film is usually an accurate image and can help by showing small details of clothes, objects, people's expressions, etc.	A photograph or film can be posed or taken from a particular angle, but also it is literally a snapshot – it shows one moment but does not show before/after or tell you if this scene was typical of the wider situation.
Visual sources (drawing, painting, cartoon)	These often indicate people's feelings and ideas – a peaceful situation, an angry crowd, a wealthy person, hope for the future, etc.	We do not know whether the details shown are true or imagined, or whether the general public shared the feelings of the artist.
A secondary source (a book by an historian)	The historian would study a wide range of sources to look at both sides of an issue, before and after, and get as full a picture as possible; this should be a very accurate source.	The historian could find it hard to agree with the views of the people at the time or his attitude to an event might be affected by knowledge of what happened later.

Here is an example question.

> Which of Sources D and F is the most useful to the historian who is enquiring about people's reactions to Simpson's use of anaesthetics? (10 marks)

Activity

1. Read the three comments below on Source D. Explain why each comment is at Level 2.

Source D says that Dr Syme told the Medical Society of Edinburgh that he 'believed anaesthesia not only saved patients operated on from pain, but also from shock, and all its effects'. This information is helpful to the historian because it shows the reasons why Dr. Syme thought chloroform was an improvement in surgery.

....

Dr Syme felt so strongly about the benefits of chloroform to the patient that he was trying to convince other doctors about its importance. This could mean that he emphasises the positive aspects of chloroform and doesn't mention any problems.

....

Dr Syme is talking about his own experiences so the details can be trusted as he would remember them clearly.

....

2. Now complete the paragraphs below to turn them into Level 3 comments about Source F.

The details in Source F which help the historian who wants to know about people's

reactions towards Simpson and anaesthetics are ....

....

because ....

....

The source is a drawing of the event and therefore it is reliable/unreliable because ....

....

So the overall usefulness of this source is strong/weak because ....

....

Hint

Notice that you were only given one line for a description of the source content. Don't waste time repeating or describing the source; it's what you say about how the historian would use that content which matters.

The table below lists four sources.

3. Fill in the rest of the table to show what sort of information you could get from each source and how the nature or reliability of the source would affect its usefulness to the historian.

Source	Possible information to help the historian	Aspects of reliability that strengthen or weaken the evidence
A diary from a patient who has been one of the first to receive chloroform	This would provide a lot of information about the patient's worries and feelings before and after the operation but not about the details of the operation because the patient would be asleep.	The patient's attitude would probably be affected by whether the operation had gone well.
A newspaper report about the death of Hannah Greener		The newspaper might want to blame the doctor without knowing whether the wrong dose of chloroform had been given.
A doctor's memoirs where he remembers the old operations without anaesthetics	This would provide lots of details that could be used to show how much surgery changed as a result of anaesthetics.	
A history book called *Great Medical Discoveries*		

3B Protest, law and order

Look at the following example question that asks you to examine sources.

Which of Sources C and D is more useful to the historian who is enquiring into how united the miners were during the strike in 1984? Explain your answer, using Sources C and D. (10 marks)

Activity

1. Read the two comments on Sources C and D. Beneath each comment, explain why it is Level 2.

Source D is useful to the historian as it gives you more examples of how they were united such as they ran a kitchen and that they made sure at Christmas all the families 'got a turkey and a tenner'. They also helped each other and made sure that 'nobody starved or froze'.

....

Source C is more useful because it is not one-sided and it gives you both sides of the story and Source D is only about how the miners helped each other.

....

2. Now complete the paragraphs below to write a Level 3 answer. Use **BOTH** the content of the sources and their reliability to decide which you think is the best source for a historian enquiring into how united the miners were during the strike in 1984.

Source D gives examples of how miners were united such as ....

....

However this source is less reliable because it is only giving us ....

....

Source C gives examples of how the miners were united such as ....

....

But it also gives us the other side of the story with the example of ....

....

Therefore I think for this enquiry that Source .... is the most useful because ....

....

....

3. The table below lists six sources. Fill in the rest of the table to show what sort of information you could get from each source and how the nature of the source would affects its usefulness to the historian.

Source	Possible information to help the historian	Aspects of reliability that strengthen or weaken the evidence
A newspaper that supported the miners	Examples of why the miners were on strike and what action they took	
A diary entry from a miner who did not take part in the strike		It is only one person's perspective
An interview 30 years later with a miner who had supported the strike		Some of the details may not be reliable as the person is recollecting events from a long time ago
The BBC news coverage of the Miners' Strike	It will give a clear visual image of events	
The diary of a member of Thatcher's government		It will give a detailed account of the views of the government

Judgement questions

Unit 3 is always based around an enquiry. The background information at the start of the Sources Booklet identifies the key issue. The final question in Unit 3 will always ask you to make a judgement on that issue.

This question carries 16 marks and it is very similar to the 16-mark questions in Unit 1 and Unit 2. For example, it could be about the importance of a person or a factor, it could be about causes or consequences, it could be about change, and so on.

How do I answer judgement questions?

The question is often phrased as a statement and you are asked: 'How far do you agree?' You need to plan an answer that looks at both sides – reasons for agreeing and reasons for disagreeing – but you still need to analyse the question in the same way as you would for the questions in Units 1 and 2. For example:

- identify the topic

- check the time frame

- think about what angle or focus is expected.

The big difference is that Unit 3 is the source paper, and therefore you need to use both your own knowledge and the specified sources in your answer.

How will I be marked?

The mark scheme is very similar to the one used in Units 1 and 2 but look carefully at the requirements to **use the sources and your own knowledge**. Own knowledge could be used to give extra detail about something mentioned in a source, or to bring in a totally new point.

Level	Marks	Descriptor
2	5–8	Answer offers a judgement and links this to details from the sources and/or own knowledge.
3	9–10	Answer makes a judgement, showing how evidence from the sources or own knowlege supports or challenges that judgement.
	11–12	Answer makes a judgement, showing how evidence from sources **and** own knowledge supports or challenges that judgement.
4	13–16	Answer weighs the evidence from sources **and** own knowledge on both sides of the issue, showing clearly how the judgement has been reached.

Once again, there is no expected 'right' answer – just make sure you use the sources and your own knowledge in your answer.

Spelling, punctuation and grammar

In question 5 there are up to 3 additional marks for spelling, punctuation and grammar. The table below shows how you will be marked.

0 marks	Errors severely hinder the meaning of the response or students do not spell, punctuate or use the rules of grammar within the context of the demands of the question.
Level 1: Threshold performance 1 mark	Students spell, punctuate and use the rules of grammar with reasonable accuracy in the context of the demands of the question. Any errors do not hinder meaning in the response. Where required, they use a limited range of specialist terms appropriately.
Level 2: Intermediate performance 2 marks	Students spell, punctuate and use the rules of grammar with considerable accuracy and general control of meaning in the context of the demands of the question. Where required, they use a good range of specialist terms with facility.
Level 3: High performance 3 marks	Students spell, punctuate and use the rules of grammar with consistent accuracy and effective control of meaning in the context of the demands of the question. Where required, they use a wide range of specialist terms adeptly and with precision.

Here is an exam-style question that asks you to come to a judgement.

> 'The development of anaesthetics was a major advance in surgery'. Explain how far you agree with this statement, using your own knowledge, sources C, E and F and any other sources you find helpful. (16 marks)

The mark scheme says that a Level 2 answer offers a judgement on the issue and links it to relevant details. At this level the answer will often go through each of the sources in turn making comments like:

a. Source C shows that the use of anaesthetics was successful, so this supports the idea in the question

b. Source E is about a girl who died, so this source is against the idea

c. Source F shows that people thought Simpson was wonderful so this source supports it.

There are two problems with this sort of approach. The first is that each time the answer refers to a source, it **says** whether the source is for or against the idea that anaesthetics led to advances in surgery. A Level 3 answer must explain this – you need to **show how** the details support or challenge the idea.

Activity

1. Rewrite each of the sentences, **explaining** whether each one supports or challenges the idea (not just saying it) and including **detail** from the source to back up your comments. The first one has been done for you.

   a. Source C shows that the use of anaesthetics was successful

   because a painful operation had been carried out with perfect results. The surgeon's view fits with the idea that the use of anaesthetics was an advance in surgery because he says it could destroy pain, which he describes as 'a very great thing'.

   b. Source E is about a girl who died ....

   ....

   ....

   c. Source F says people thought Simpson was wonderful ....

   ....

   ....

The second problem with going through each of the sources in turn is that the essay does not build up a clear argument. It is much better to put together all the points where you agree with the statement and then cover all the points where you don't agree.

Five minutes spent planning means that the essay can move smoothly from one point to the next, instead of jumping around and having to use asterisks to go back and add in extra comments.

Activity

2. Complete the planning table for this question. Don't worry if you have to leave a box blank because all the points from a source seem to be on one side of the issue.

Evidence	Points to support the statement	Points to challenge the statement
Source C		
Source E		
Source F		
Own knowledge	Ended the problem of pain – people more willing to have operations done instead of treating surgery as a last resort. Patient did not need to be held down – less risk of accidents. Surgeon able to work a little more slowly and take time to do the operation carefully.	Problem of deaths from chloroform – no way to measure the dose properly. There was opposition to the use of chloroform from some doctors and also from religious groups. The death rate went up because surgeons tried more complex operations inside the body but did not understood about germs, so they put dirty hands and instruments into an open wound, and patients who survived the operation often died from infection later.

3. Now rearrange your evidence so that your essay has a logical structure to it, as below:

○ Evidence to show that the development of anaesthetics was a major advance in surgery:

- The problem of pain and its effects on surgery

  Source .... Own knowledge ....

- The benefits of anaesthetics

  Source .... Own knowledge ....

○ Evidence to show that the development of anaesthetics was not a major advance in surgery

- Problems using ether and chloroform

  Source .... Own knowledge ....

- Reasons for opposition

  Source .... Own knowledge ....

○ Your judgement

....

....

Activity

Below is a student answer with a number of spelling, punctuation and grammar errors. Read the answer and:

- underline any spelling mistakes

- circle any errors of punctuation or grammar

- rewrite the answer with accurate spelling, punctuation and grammar on a separate sheet of paper.

one of the main problems caused by anethetics were infection because surgens could perform more complex operations with anethetics and also operations were done for smaller problems as said in source x sepsis occurred. the use of anethetics in operations before anticeptics were developed is known as the black period of sergery due to high death rates, source x shows the problems of infection saying 'infection and gangrene spread through the wards'. also because more complex operations occured the problem of blood loose became something that killed many people, also doses were not decided on so many patents like hannah greener died on overdose, also ether and cloroform had problems, ether was extreamely flamable and irritated lungs and cloroform could stop the heart, also as source y shows the army were against using cloroform as they felt men should bite the bullet. on the other hand anethetics did improve sergery, as source z shows many patents would died from shock before anethetics so most people would not have operations, this is also in source w were it says the greatest danger was pain and some patents did not recover and anethetics offered hope to patents which suggests it was a benefit. overal I think that without anethetics sergery may not of developed to the modern tecniques used today like anticeptics as the high death rates would of prevented progress.

3B Protest, law and order

Here is an exam-style question that asks you to come to a judgement.

> 'For protestors the media was a useful way to gain support.'
>
> How far do you agree with this view? Explain your answer, using your own knowledge, Sources A, B and F and any other sources you find helpful. (16 marks)

The mark scheme says that Level 2 answers offer a judgement on the issue and link it to the relevant details. Answers at Level 2 will often simply go through each of the sources in turn making comments like:

- Source A is a leaflet so this was a way the suffragettes got their views across.

- Source B is a letter in a newspaper by someone against the suffragettes so the media could also be used against them.

- Source F says that they wanted to get to the BBC because they wanted people to know what was going on.

There are two problems with this sort of approach. The first problem is that each time the answer refers to a source, it **says** whether the source is for or against the idea that the media was a useful way for the protestors to get support. Level 3 answers must **explain** with details from the sources to agree, disagree or even partly agree with the statement.

Activity

1. Firstly complete the planning table below for the above question. Don't worry if you have to leave a box blank because all the points from some sources may support or challenge the statement.

Evidence	Points to support the statement	Points to challenge the statement
Source A		
Source B		
Source F		
Own knowledge		

The second main problem with going through each of the sources in turn is that your essay does not build up a clear argument. It is much better to group the sources so that all those that support the statement are together, as are all those that challenge the statement.

2. Now rearrange your evidence so that your essay has a logical structure to it:

- Evidence to show that the media **WAS** a useful way of gaining support

  - Source .... • Source ....
- Evidence to show the media **WAS NOT** useful way to gain support

  - Source .... Own knowledge ....
  - Source .... Own knowledge ....

3. On separate piece of paper write your full essay for the question. Start your essay clearly with the following statement:

   I think that the media did/did not/partly played a useful way to gaining support for the protest because

Activity

Below is a student answer with a number of spelling, punctuation and grammar errors. Read the answer and:

- underline any spelling mistakes

- circle any errors of punctuation or grammar

- rewrite the answer with accurate spelling, punctuation and grammar on a separate sheet of paper.

during the miners strikes there was some cases of vilence like the battle of orgreave and a taxi driver killed when taking a miner to work. it was said in the battle of orgreve that the miners' used vilence against the police eg in source x it says police offisers were attacked with bricks, it is also implied in source w that miners using vilence and the bbc shown scens of miners' attacking police. a taxi driver was kill on the way to a pit when taking a working miner there, this made the public angry and resulted in miners loosing support from the public as they thought the miners was becoming too militent, this is also coroborated by source z as it shows how public opinion was firm against the miners. scabs were often beaten up and ostercised and this angered the public as they felt people shouldn't be beaten up purley for doing there job. years after the strikes the bbc admited that the minors did not attack the police first at orgreave and infact the bbc had broadcasted the events in the wrong order, this is coroborated by source y as it says the police charge provoked the missile throwing

Units 1 and 2

Inference: 1A Medicine through time (pages 7–8)

1 b) and d). Answer A is based on comment b).

2 Comment d) could be supported by explaining that the woman in A is working from a 'recipe' book whereas B says nurses carry out 'the treatment prescribed by a doctor'.

3–5 Read the feedback under Answer B.

6 Your improved answer should mention details in A showing the woman and her maid making their own medicine whereas Rathbone is writing in B to several nurses saying they are 'trained and skilled workers' suggesting there is a group of them – presumably at a hospital. Do not include the comment about Florence Nightingale, which is not based on the source.

Inference: 1B Crime and punishment (pages 9–10)

1 b) and d). Answer A is based on comment b).

2 Comment d) could be supported by the use of the word 'riot' in A and the claim it is 'necessary' to use military force suggests it is an emergency whereas in B the police already have the equipment which suggests it is normal duties.

3–5 Read the feedback under Answer B.

6 Your improved answer should mention the use of military force in A compared to the defensive wall that can be seen in B. You should not include the comment about police uniform, which is not based on the source.

Inference: 2B American West (pages 11–12)

1 d)

2 1-B; 2-A; 3-B; 4-B; 5-B

3 Your answer should include a clearly supported inference from the source.

4 Answer A is Level 2 – 4 marks. The inference about religion is supported directly from the source 'size of the temple'. The answer also does not need own knowledge about Brigham Young, the Perpetual Emigration Fund and the establishment of Utah.

Answer B gets 0 marks. This response is the student's own knowledge and makes no use of the source at all.

Inference: 2C Life in Germany (pages 13–14)

1 b) and e)

2 1-A; 2-B; 3-A; 4-B; 5-B

3 Your answer should include a clearly supported inference from the source.

4 Answer A is Level 2 – 3 marks. There is a valid inference about a method of Nazi government's control with book-burnings of books. The inferences about "busy areas" and "ceremony" could have been supported more directly from the source to give a 4-mark answer. The answer does not need own knowledge about censorship and the Nazi government's control of other areas.

Answer B gets 0 marks. This response is the student's own knowledge and makes no use of the source at all.

Causation: 1A Medicine through time (pages 16–17)

1 You should have underlined the sentence starting: 'However, it was difficult…back to his original research' and the phrase 'but they needed to get funding'.

2 ..he did not do any further experiments and so the usefulness of penicillin in medicine was not fully developed.
..because it was killed by stomach acid and therefore it could not be used to treat any internal infection or illness.
..because nobody saw it as a priority to develop the mass production of penicillin until the American government was worried about lots of casualties in the Second World War.

3 1B; 2D; 3A; 4C.

Causation: 1B Crime and punishment (pages 18–19)

1 You should have underlined the sentences 'Smuggling was usually carried out at night….in the dark; There was no police… catch the smugglers'. And the phrases 'most people would not inform the authorities. However, the smugglers could also be very violent …afraid of them'.

2 ..such as the bays and coves all along the coast, especially when it was done at night, in the dark and it was difficult to see what was happening.
..was because many people benefited from buying luxury goods at cheap prices from the smugglers.
..because smuggling gangs could be violent so people were afraid to make them angry.

3 1C; 2A; 3D; 4B.

Causation: 2B American West (pages 20–21)

1 Answer A is Level 2 because it is a descriptive answer.

2 Suggested sentence endings:
i) *beliefs in the spirit world, medicine men, visions, dances, how they fought battles, having more than one wife.*
ii) *they followed buffalo herds, used tipis and sometime left the elderly behind.*
iii) *beliefs in sacred land such as the Black Hills was not understood by the whites.*
iv) *was strange as the Indians did not believe in killing the enemy and instead used counting coup to show bravery.*

Causation: 2C Life in Germany (pages 22–23)

1 Answer A is Level 2 because it is a descriptive answer.

2 Suggested sentence endings:
i) *they did not have the same rights as other Germans.*
ii) *this meant they had fewer educational opportunities , were increasingly segregated from other Germans, the marriage laws were used to create a "pure" race.*
iii) *German Jewish culture and their livelihoods were being physically destroyed.*
iv) *Nazi racial ideas could be implemented.*
v) *people lived in fear of their neighbours informing on them.*

Consequence: 1A Medicine through time (pages 25–26)

1 1C; 2D; 3B; 4A

2 Relevant: 2, 3, 4, 5; Not relevant: 1, 6.

3 ..*structure of the body very accurately. This helped doctors because they could study it and improve their understanding of anatomy even if they didn't see a dissection carried out on a real body.*
…*Harvey's book … important because medical training was all based on Galen's ideas, so if people began to challenge those ideas and experiment for themselves they would develop more accurate knowledge.*
Once these new ideas ….easy for doctors to keep up with new ideas because new ideas could be printed in books and everyone could quickly buy a copy and talk about them.

Consequence: 1B Crime and punishment (pages 27–28)

1 1D; 2C; 3A; 4B

2 Relevant: 1, 2, 4, 5; Not relevant: 3.

3 …*they were taught to knit and sew so that they could earn a wage when they were released, instead of going back to crime.*
… *a book she wrote and as she gave evidence to parliament which publicised the situation and her ideas.*
…*had been accepted and better treatment and religious teaching while in prison was being used to help lead the prisoners to repent about their crimes.*

Consequence: 2B The American West (pages 29–30)

1 Level 2: A, B, D, E, F, G, J; Level 3: C, H, I

2 … *those that discovered gold.*
…*meant returning home or carrying on travelling in the hope of finding gold.*
…*violence, claim-jumping, lawlessness, corrupt miners courts, vigilante committees.*
… *the growth of business and development of a mining industry, new machinery, families joining the miners led to new, permanent towns, the growth of San Francisco, increased USA's role in world trade.*

3 Suggestions:
1. White men moved onto the land.
2. Railroad companies wanted Indians and buffalo removed.
3. The US government made the 1861 Fort Wise Treaty.
4. The US government wanted the Indians on smaller reservations.
5. Many Indians refused to accept these changes.

Consequence: 2C Life in Germany (pages 31–32)

1 Level 2: A, D, E, G, J
Level 3: B, C, F, H, I

2 … *pensioners and the middle class.*
… *they were on fixed incomes or they lost their savings.*
… *some businessmen, people in debt.*
… *they could invest, take over failing businesses, their debts were wiped out.*
… *people lost trust in the government, Hitler saw it as an opportunity to try and take power.*

3 Suggestions:
1. More of the German people became afraid of communism.
2. Hitler could use this to increase fear of communism.
3. It was used to introduce emergency powers.
4. The Communist Party (KPD) was banned.
5. It led to the passing of the Enabling Act.

Role: 1A Medicine through time (pages 34–35)

1 Comment about Germ Theory is Level 2, a description of what Pasteur did; comment about X-rays is Level 3, it explains how X-rays could help in medicine, doesn't explain how other machines helped; comment about Crick & Watson is Level 2, it briefly describes the situation. Overall it is a low Level 3 (9 marks) as only one example of science and technology is used to show how medical understanding was changed.

2 …*once people understood how disease was caused they could use that knowledge to start to develop effective ways of preventing and treating illness.*
… *CAT scans, MRI scans and ultrasound scans can show if there* is something wrong with the organs and tissues inside the body, while an EEG monitor can check whether the brain is working properly.
… *Crick and Watson discovered the structure of DNA. This meant scientists could begin to identify which bits of each gene is faulty when people have genetic conditions.*

4 1D; 2A; 3E; 4B; 5C

Role: 1B Crime (pages 36–37)

1 Comment about old crimes (theft) is Level 2, a description of 'old' crimes involving technology; comment about new crimes (drink-driving, computers etc) is Level 2, a description of 'new' crimes involving technology; comment about technology and the police is mainly Level 2 (description) but the point about using computers to check fingerprints and keep records is Level 3, a brief example of how technology helps the police to do their work. Overall it is a low Level 3 (9 marks) with several examples to show that technology has made a difference to crime and police work but only one example actually explains how the technology helps.

2 …*it is easier for the criminal to get far away very quickly and they can also carry bigger or more goods than if they were on foot.*
… *crimes such as speeding, drink-driving and driving without a licence didn't exist before cars were made because these laws were made in order to make roads safer.*
… *the computer can store more records in less space than paper records but also a computer can match details very quickly.*
… *special squads to deal with car crime or computer hacking.*

4 1E; 2D; 3B; 4C; 5A

Role: 2B The American West (pages 38–39)

1 The first four lines from '*There were*' until '*damaged their farm land*.'

3 Wind pumps & Turkey Red Wheat are not relevant to this question.

Role: 2C Nazi Germany (pages 40–41)

1 The first four lines from 'In the very early years' until 'votes to get into power.'

3 Munich (Beer Hall Putsch), The Eternal Jew & Hitler Youth military units are not relevant to this question.

Evaluation: 1A Medicine through time (pages 46–49)

1 *Orange*: Explain how each of 3 or 4 points was a reason for the delay
Scales: Weigh up similarities and differences
Iceberg: Explain why chance was important but also explain other reasons
Scales: Weigh up change and continuity
Orange: Explain a range of consequences and explain which was the most important
Orange: Explain a range of reasons

2 1D; 2A; 3E; 4C; 5B

4 The correct comment is: Top Level 3, 12 marks

5 Cause: Similarity in *imbalance of four humours* and *miasma*; Difference in *religion* and *spontaneous generation*.
Treatment: Similarity in *bleeding and purging*, and *herbal remedies*; Difference in *trying to get poison out of buboes* and *patent medicines*.
Prevention: Similarity in *burning*; Difference in *flagellants, keeping air moving, isolation, burning tar* and *smoking cigars*.

Government action: Similarity in *order to clean up towns*; Difference in *order of days of prayer and fasting*.

Evaluation: 1B Crime and punishment (pages 50–54)

1 *Orange*: Explain how each of three or four points was a reason for its abolition.
Scales: Weigh up similarities and differences
Iceberg: Explain why car crime was a problem but also consider other crimes
Scales: Weigh up change and continuity
Scales: Weigh up the work of Howard and Fry
Scales: Weigh up aspects of change in the two periods.

2 1D; 2C; 3E; 4B; 5A

4 The correct comment is: Top Level 3, 12 marks.

5 Nature: Similarity in *luxury goods smuggled, cigarettes and alcohol smuggled* and *tax avoidance*; Difference in *animals poached, illegal goods smuggled*
Methods: Similarity in *organised gangs*; Difference in *carried out at night, no specific time, technology*
Public attitudes: Similarity in *sympathy*; Difference in *respectable members of society, hostility to organised smuggling or tax evasion*

Evaluation: 2B The American West (pages 55–58)

1 From: '*In 1865 after*' to '*at Sedalia*'; '*Therefore*' to '*long drive*'; '*Then more ranchers*' to '*from Texas*'; '*Cowboys could now,*' to '*their work.*'

2 *In 1865 after the Civil War; 5 million; John Iliff and Texas Longhorns; Glidden and barbed wire; 1869 first trans-continental railroad.*

3 a) …*because*…; …*so*…
   b) … *this meant that*…; …*therefore*…

5 *Donner Party; Manifest Destiny; San Francisco; wind pumps; barbed wire*

6 The first four lines from '*Before the coming*' until '*being cannibals*' are irrelevant.

7 The feedback should be in this order: A, D, B, C

Evaluation: 2C Life in Germany (pages 59–62)

1 From '*The 3K's*' to '*use make-up*' and from '*Many women lost*' to '*in factories*'

2 *loan details; 3K's; special medals*

3 a) … *because*… ; … *so*…
   b) … *because*… ; … *this meant that*…

5 [indicate what they should underline]

6 The first four lines from '*Soon after*' until '*Germans and Jews illegal*' are irrelevant.

7 Feedback should be in this order: B, D, C, A

8 B; D; C; A

Unit 3

Inference and portrayal: 3A Surgery (pages 73–74)

1 …*the room has space organised for a number of people to watch.*
… *the fact that people are wearing ordinary clothes, there are no surgical gloves or gowns, the instruments are washed, not sterilised.*
… *the fact that ordinary knives are used, there is limited equipment because people are needed to hold the patient down.*

2 Answer A is Level 1 because it describes the room without making an inference and the inferences about pain, speed and infection cannot be supported from the source.

3 The phrase '*worthy of experiment*' and the sentence '*Saying 'just prepared''* to '*tested it before*' show how words create the impression that chloroform was new.

4 The sentence '*The idea that it was dangerous*' to '*rabbits had died*' shows how the author used details to suggest that chloroform was dangerous.

5 …*brave to the point of rashness.*
…*how Simpson wanted to rush eagerly and not think about whether the mixture is dangerous*

Inference and portrayal: 3B Protest (pages 75–76)

1 … *the source says this suffragette was 'thrown down', her 'hair was seized' and her 'head bumping on the stairs'. She was also subjected to 'forcible feeding', was 'handcuffed again' and 'flung down the steps.'*
… *the source saying that the prison authorities were 'encouraged by the government'.*
… *these examples about how they were treated.*

2 Answer A is Level 2 because it uses details from the source to support a valid comment

3 The comment '*the way they were treated the prison staff was harsh.*'

4 To do this answers must give at least one direct quote from the source of an example of how the suffragettes were treated.

5 *riot and disturb*; horde

6 *uses high-bred in a sarcastic way; how he thinks money should be saved*

Cross referencing: 3A Surgery (pages 78–79)

1 … it *considers the reliability of the information.*
… *it shows how the reliability of the source makes it strong evidence and means the historian can use its information to reach a judgement.*

2 Source content: Source B – Simpson didn't create the anaesthetic and Simpson tested the anaesthetic. Source D – Simpson suggested chloroform be used in operations and Dr Syme said Simpson was right – it prevented pain and saved patients from shock.
Similarity: Source B – Simpson is experimenting to find a way of relieving pain.
Difference: Source B – Simpson used other people's ideas. Source D – Simpson is given the credit for the use of anaesthetics.
Reliability: Source B – Speaking from personal knowledge, no reason to lie. Source D – Speaking from personal knowledge, has added weight because admits he changed his mind but was trying to persuade others to use chloroform as well.

Cross referencing: 3B Protest (pages 80–81)

1 Answer B is Level 2 because it matches the detail of the sources to find examples of support.

2 Answer C is Level 3 because it evaluates the sources for reliability.

3 Source content: Source E – A painting of the Poll Tax riots in Trafalgar Square showing the police and rioters attacking each other. Source F – A description of the fighting between the police and protestors and details of what happened elsewhere.

Points of similarity: Source E – Both the protestors and police are using violence, there is a police van, a fire bomb going off and the police are using batons, shields and horses. Source F – Says the police are attacking and the rioters are fighting back using batons, shields and had horses.

Points of difference: Source E – This is only about what happened in Trafalgar Square and you can't tell who is the most to blame for the violence. Source F – Gives the impression that the rioters were fighting back but it also includes details about other things the protestors did outside of Trafalgar Square such as looting shops and smashing windows.

Points about reliability: Source E – The artist does not seem to be supporting either the police or the protestors. Source F – An eye-witness account from personal knowledge. A demonstrator might give a non-balanced view but it does include the violence of both the police and demonstrators.

Source evaluation: 3A Surgery (pages 85–86)

1 This explains the value of the source content but doesn't say how it helps the historian in their enquiry.
This is considering an aspect of reliability but doesn't show how the information in the source helps the historian.
This is considering an aspect of reliability but doesn't show how the information in the source helps the historian.

2 …that people are coming to see a statue of Simpson being unveiled.
… it suggests many people admired him and wanted to honour him.
… we do not know if details are accurate, such as the size of the crowd.
… we cannot assume from the picture that he was widely admired without knowing if the size of the crowd is accurate.

3 Newspaper report: This would give details of her operation and what went wrong and also tell us about public reaction to her death.
Doctor's memoirs: The doctor would be looking back at the period, knowing how anaesthetics improved surgery – this might affect the way he talks about the situation, possibly exaggerating to stress how important anaesthetics were.
A history book called _Great Medical Discoveries_: The book would give information about what was discovered, how it affected operations, and how both surgeons and the public reacted. It would also be able to put events into the context of other events at the time or show what happened later. The historian should have researched a wide range of evidence and weighed up the reliability of sources in order to form his judgement.

Source evaluation: 3B Protest (pages 87–88)

1 Level 2 because it makes a decision by showing which source's information helps the historian more.
Level 2 because it makes a decision by showing which source is more reliable.

2 Here are some suggestions:
… the union's area executive ensured that every family got a turkey and a tenner.
… examples of how people supported each other.
… '10,000 strong', 'mass meetings' and 'marches'
… the example of two "scab" miners.
…Source C gives examples of how the miners and their communities were both united but also examples of division.

3 Newspaper: Possible information – Examples of why the miners were on strike and what action they took; Reliability – It will only give the miners point of view and be biased against the police and government
Miner's diary: Possible information – The thoughts and opinions of a miner who was against the strike; Reliability – It is only one person's perspective
Interview: Possible information – It is from someone first-hand who experienced the strike; Reliability – Some of the details may not be reliable as the person is recollecting events from a long time ago
BBC news: Possible information – It will give a clear visual image of events; Reliability – It is likely to represent the events in a fair way and show the views and actions of both the authorities and the miners
MPs diary: Possible information – It will give a detailed account on the views of the government; Reliability – Government ministers often publish their diaries and so it may omit certain information and highlight other aspects

Judgement: 3A Surgery (pages 90–91)

1 b …which shows that the use of anaesthetics was not always a good thing. It is a useful reminder that they couldn't control the correct dosage even though they only gave her one-third of a normal dose. It shows that anaesthetics did not solve all the problems of surgery.
c … which shows that by 1877 most people had accepted anaesthetics and the problems had been solved. The fact that so many people came to see Simpson's statue being unveiled suggests they thought he had achieved a great thing and they saw anaesthetics as progress.
2 Source C: Support – In both operations perfect and satisfactory results; Challenge – Only two examples – not enough to support the claim that it was a major advance in surgery.
Source E: Support – Operation was painful so surgeon wanted to use chloroform – expected it to help; Challenge – Difficult to be exact about dosage; patient had a stroke and died.
Source F: Support – Statue of Simpson shows people felt he deserved honour; crowd suggests he was admired; Challenge – No information given to say who chose to erect the statue – doesn't necessarily show public opinion, or it could be in recognition of something else he did.

Judgement: 3B Protest (page 92)

1 Source A: Support – The suffragettes used leaflets to spread their opinions
Source B: Challenge – This is a letter to a newspaper to try and raise opposition to the suffragettes
Source F: Support – The protestors wanted the BBC to put their point of view across